Rethinking the Education of Deaf Students

Theory and Practice from a Teacher's Perspective

Sue Livingston

Foreword by James E. Tucker

Heinemann
Portsmouth, NH

Heinemann
A division of Reed Elsevier Inc.
361 Hanover Street
Portsmouth, NH 03801-3912

Offices and agents throughout the world.

Library of Congress Cataloging-in-Publication Data
Livingston, Sue.
    Rethinking the education of deaf students: theory and practice
from a teacher's perspective / Sue Livingston : foreword by James E.
Tucker.
      p. cm.
    Includes bibliographical references and index.
    ISBN 0-435-07236-6
    1. Deaf—Education—United States—English language. 2. Children,
Deaf—United States—Language. 3. American Sign Language—Study and
teaching. I. Title.
    HV2469.E5L58 1997   97-3501
    371.91'2—dc21   CIP

Editor: Scott Mahler
Production: Renée Le Verrier
Cover Design: Catherine Hawkes
Manufacturing: Louise Richardson

Printed in the United States of America on acid-free paper.
Docutech T & C 2007

Contents

Foreword

This book reflects Sue Livingston's lifelong passion in exploring new and innovative ways of promoting the development of language, reading, and writing abilities of Deaf students. As her graduate student at New York University in 1982-1983, I saw her determination to treat Deaf students as everyday human beings with an innate capacity for effortless language acquisition. Her insightful classroom lectures a decade ago are now translated into this book, complete with criticism of Deaf Education's pathologically driven ideologies, as well as a precious collection of teaching strategies that have successfully facilitated reading and writing growth in Deaf students of all ages.

The thrust of this book is that language acquisition and the learning of reading and writing are motivated by meaning-making and meaning-sharing. This simple but powerful concept has enormous implication for how teachers of Deaf students, administrators of schools for Deaf students, and professors of Deaf Education should educate Deaf students, develop school budgets, design programs, and train future teachers. Livingston's tenets require a complete overhaul of the Deaf Education system as we know and understand it today.

To ensure students' quest for meaning, Livingston proposes that Deaf students use American Sign Language (ASL) to gain full, clear, and direct access to information "through the air." This and the need for a community of ASL users is in direct conflict with the current maddening rush to isolate Deaf students in local public schools. This is also in direct conflict with disastrous Oral-only and Simultaneous Communication methods. This is also in direct conflict with educators' insistence that curricula be watered down for Deaf students and taught piecemeal.

Livingston also proposes that educators treat Deaf students no differently from non-Deaf students. Deaf students are perfectly capable of achieving fluency in reading and writing like their non-Deaf counterparts. Being Deaf is not to be magnified and then used as an excuse for delaying reading and writing activities for Deaf children. Rather, possessing an understanding of linguistic and cultural issues is essential to believing that all Deaf students can and will become better readers and writers.

In Chapters 3, 4, and 5, Livingston revels in the joy of watching Deaf students grow as readers and writers through the use of ASL and English. There are no gimmicks in fostering this development. To become a successful reader, one must enjoy reading and spend time practicing reading. To become a successful writer, one must enjoy writing and spend time practicing writing. And, reciprocally, through meaningful reading and writing, Deaf students grow as learners, as well as users of ASL and English. She eloquently explains strategies step by step and shares students' responses to reading and writing samples with us. Student learning and achievement throughout this book are embraced and celebrated.

Having this manuscript in hand, I have the good fortune of sharing it with teachers and administrators at the Frederick and Columbia campuses of The Maryland School for the Deaf before this book reaches bookstores and school and home libraries. Strategies outlined in this book have been field-tested and were successful. Teachers with a larger arsenal of effective strategies become more exemplary in their work—their students are, of course, the direct beneficiaries of this.

Sue Livingston has challenged our preconceived notions of how Deaf students grow as language users, readers, and writers. It is hoped that her educational theories, successful pedagogical practices, and personal knowledge of Deaf and hard-of-hearing students' cognitive and linguistic abilities will stimulate our collective minds and push us forward in our thinking that in every Deaf student is a potentially voracious reader and an accomplished writer.

James E. Tucker, Superintendent
The Maryland School for the Deaf

Acknowledgments

To the hundreds of students I have learned from over the past twenty-five years at the School for the Deaf—Junior High School 47, LaGuardia Community College, The St. Joseph's School for the Deaf, and The Maryland School for the Deaf;

to the faculty at these schools whose questions and concerns about the education of Deaf students guided my thinking throughout the writing of this book, and to Pat Martin, Superintendent of The St. Joseph's School for the Deaf, who spurred me on to do extended in-service work with her motivated teachers;

to Fern Khan at the Bank Street College of Education for the opportunity to teach "Teaching Reading and Writing to Deaf Students," which forced me to organize my teaching experiences into book-like form;

to John Mayher of New York University who, in my imagination, was reading right along with me as I was writing, and whose comments made this a much better book;

to Doris Naiman for advice to "Say it up front and directly";

to Nancy Swaiko for the time and effort given to painstakingly detail what works and what doesn't for her as a teacher and for her ever-so-kind words of encouragement;

to Peter and Jenna for never asking and to Erva and Grace for . . . just everything;

and finally, to my Spring '93 CSE and ENG students who said, "You should write a book":

Thank you.

Preface

The profession of educating Deaf students has been and continues to be mired in theoretical and methodological misconceptions. Albeit with every good intention, educators have mistakenly viewed the education of their students as being vastly different from the education of hearing students. Although there are differences, to be sure, they have been taken to far outweigh the similarities that exist between Deaf and hearing learners and have been magnified to create a system of education that smacks of remediation and repair. For far too long, the fact that we teach Deaf students has precluded the more important fact that we teach, first and foremost, human learners who just happen to be Deaf.

Although the distinction may seem subtle, its implication is not. When we teach Deaf students, we codify and reconstruct. We codify the English language in signs and teach it in an orderly, simple-to-complex, piecemeal manner "through the air" and through adapted readings and skill-and-drill writing activities to make it "easier" for them. The thinking is that Deaf students are so different from other learners that their language needs to be unnaturally taught as opposed to naturally caught. The primary goal of education is teaching and learning English in its signed, printed and, hoped for, spoken forms; the core theoretical assumption is that English needs to be more or less under students' belts before subject-area learning or "real work" can begin. When content is taught, it is English-language–driven, whereby the structures and functions of the English used in its teaching are valued more than the contexts they service.

In contrast, when we teach human learners who happen to be Deaf, we do not need to "fix" language. We use the rich, natural sign language of the American Deaf Community in natural contexts and teach much the way exemplary, whole language teachers of hearing students teach reading and writing and subject-area reading and writing. The primary goal of education is the acquisition of understanding or the making and sharing of meaning in the various disciplines that co-occurs with, supports, and is supported by the acquisition of American Sign Language (ASL) and English. ASL and English are embedded in content and inseparable from it.

Subscribing to the latter view of Deaf students, the major premise of this book is that if Deaf students are immersed in ASL, reading, writing, and subject-area reading and writing, and if teaching/learning is kept whole and meaning-driven—as will be explained and exemplified—then ASL, English, and subject-area understandings will be learned reciprocally. Just as language and thought are inextricably linked, so are language and content.

My goal in writing this book is to address the dire need for educators to rethink their views of Deaf students and, in so doing, the theoretical underpinnings of their teaching methodologies. As a teacher of Deaf students for twenty-five years, I know firsthand how difficult change is, but I also know the frustration that grows from working within systems that do not work. Without a doubt, the pain of change is much more worth the stultification of daily sameness and ineffectiveness.

By change, I certainly do not mean that all teachers of Deaf students need to stop what they are doing—in my travels I have seen some exceptional teachers—nor are my suggestions meant to be viewed as written in stone or "quick fixes." If while you are reading this, you stop and think, "Interesting" or "I never thought of that," and if you share your thinking with a colleague, that dialogue, which needs to be established before change can meaningfully happen, will be reason enough for my having written this book.

Chapter One

What Has Gone Wrong in the Education of Deaf Students and Why

Two Basic Misconceptions

We Have Been Using a Sign System and Not a Sign Language

In a poignant article in the *Silent News* (1992), "the world's most popular newspaper of the Deaf," Darlene Shoemake, a Deaf graduate of Lamar University with an M.S. Degree in Deaf Education, writes of her frustration observing hearing teachers "teach down" to Deaf students.

> Hearing teachers would try to teach a lesson using Signed English, then when the Deaf child did not respond with comprehension, the teacher would simplify her English even more, thus watering down the concept she was trying to teach. . . .Really, it was the hearing teacher's English which the deaf students did not understand. . . .As a result, the deaf children that I observed were deprived of interesting and challenging content in their curriculum because the teacher could not sign the lesson in such a way that the deaf child would be able to understand it. . . .Why do hearing teachers teach to the English level of deaf students rather than teach to their level of understanding? (p. 3)

The answer to Darlene's question brings us face to face with one of the major misconceptions in our field. We have thought, and continue to think, that coding the English language with signs for individual words and morphemes will enable Deaf students to learn English. As this wishful thinking goes, Deaf students exposed to one

1

of the Signed English systems should supposedly become competent English signers, speakers, readers, and writers. For the twenty-some-odd years that Signed English systems have been in existence, however, none of this has proved true. Why is this so?

First and foremost, Signed English systems are not natural languages—they did not naturally evolve over time within a human community of users but, instead, were invented by educators. Natural languages conform to the constraints dictated by neurological and biological capacities for language expression and reception. Constraints for spoken languages are dictated by the form and function of the ears and vocal apparatus; for natural sign languages, by the form and function of the eyes and hands. Because signs are made using the large muscles of the body, it requires more time for a sign to be made than for a word to be uttered; said differently, speakers "can deliver several words in the time that an individual using the sign system delivers one sign" (Gee and Goodhart 1988, 64). Thus, the "fit" between a particular spoken language and a particular sign system, when performed simultaneously, is never quite in synch, and speakers are forced to slow down their speech to give their hands a chance to catch up. This overall slower production rate violates the natural rate of expressing propositions, or what can be thought of as underlying simple sentences or chunks of meaning to which all natural languages comply, creating signing that is "unwieldy and cumbersome" (Klima and Bellugi 1979, 193) to execute. It is only when the myriad grammatical processes inherent in ASL (e.g., use of classifier predicates, referencing locations in space) are called into play that underlying proposition rates between visual and auditory languages even out and become normal (Klima and Bellugi 1979).

It is not only the unnatural production rate that is detrimental to language learners. Even if such signing were expressed faster and "up to speed," the resultant message could still be rather meaningless to Deaf students. James Tucker, the superintendent of The Maryland School for the Deaf (MSD) who is Deaf, calls speaking and signing at the same time "grotesque to the eye," not necessarily because it is aesthetically unpleasing, but rather because the signing is too "marked," or too even or equally stressed (Wolkomir 1992). Imagine speaking a language without emphasizing some words through intonation, rhythm, and stress. It "must be like watching a kind of written language performed in the air without any periods, commas, dashes, or semicolons, and without any clues about what is important. . . ." (Hansen 1980, 254). Consider this in light of the fact that some linguists believe that about 30 percent of our understanding of speech is based on this information (Hansen 1980). In her novel *In This Sign* (1970), Joanne Greenberg writes of how members of a Deaf congregation were often caught napping ever since a new preacher, trained to sign in English, replaced a former ASL-signing preacher. It is little wonder why.

That these production characteristics do in fact put tremendous strains on reception of information has been acknowledged by Deaf adults. "Deaf people have reported to us that while they can process each item as it appears, they find it difficult to process the message content as a whole when all the information is expressed in the sign stream as sequential elements" (Bellugi 1980, 135-136). Oliver Sacks (1989) makes no bones about it: "The overloading of short-term memory and cognitive capacity that occurs with signed English in deaf adults is experienced as difficulty and strain" (p. 112). There are, then, restrictions on the kinds of input that will allow short-term memory to function effectively. Combined encoding, or speaking and signing at the same time, encumbers the workings of short-term memory because its out-of-synch nature does not allow for the meaningful chunking and subsequent processing of language in natural ways.

Johnson, Liddell, and Erting (1989) call what I have been referring to as Signed English, Sign-Supported Speech; indeed, manually coded sign systems were invented, in part, to "fortify" speech reading. They make the point, however, that the more closely teachers stick with the speech signal (e.g., using all articles, forms of the copula, verb tenses, affixes, and prepositions), the more unintelligible the signed signal will be. This makes sense because the more English-like we make our signing, the more "stretched out in time" our propositions will be, further complicating the encoding process and, thereby, the communication between teachers and students. In addition, as most teachers know but don't readily talk about, trying to preserve the sign for word/morpheme match is both "psychologically and physically overwhelming" (p. 5).

If Deaf adults experience "difficulty and strain" processing Signed English, what must it be like for children trying to learn it as if it were a natural, first language? If Signed English was able to offer children intelligible messages, the brain would have "no choice but to acquire that [code] just as the visual system has no choice but to see, and the pancreas has no choice but to operate as pancreases do" (Krashen as cited in Crawford 1991, 102). However, although there are reports of some natural acquisition of Signed English (Bornstein, Saulnier, and Hamilton, 1980, 1981; Livingston 1983; Maxwell 1987), all of these investigations point to limited competence displayed, in some cases even after years of exposure. It appears that acquiring Signed English is just as psychologically and physically overwhelming for children to decipher messages from and acquire as it is for adults to execute. These findings call into question the very foundation upon which the Total Communication movement has been built, showing firsthand that, much to hearing parents' and educators' dismay, Deaf children do not acquire Signed English as naturally as hearing children acquire spoken English. It is unfortunate that in the twenty-some-odd years that Total Communication has continued to exist, this finding has been essentially ignored.

It is likewise unfortunate that not enough attention has been given to the kind of signing that is acquired. Oliver Sacks (1989) called it "astonishing" that even though Deaf children are exposed to Signed English systems, they evolve American Sign Language (ASL)-like forms (Suty and Friel-Patti 1982; Livingston 1983; Supalla 1986; Gee and Goodhart 1988). He claims that this is testament to "an innate grammatical competence in the brain" (p. 111) that goes beyond grammars found derelict in their meaning-making duties to spontaneously create grammars that make sense presented gesturally and received visually. Gee and Goodhart (1988) describe this phenomenon as "nativization," which stipulates that without appropriate and adequate exposure to a naturally occurring language, children will innovate their own set of grammatical rules according to the innate dictates of their human biological capacity for language. "They [Deaf children] ultimately converge on ASL-like forms and an ASL-like system because, we hypothesize, this system represents the expression of the human linguistic biological capacity in the manual modality" (p. 70).

Sacks (1989) goes on to say that given the constraints inherent in processing a visual language, the unique linguistic structure of ASL *has to* evolve:

> And there is strong circumstantial support for this in the fact that all the indigenous signed languages—and there are many hundreds, all over the world, which have evolved separately and independently wherever there are groups of deaf people—*all* indigenous signed languages have much the same spatial structure. None of them resembles signed English or signed speech in the least. All have, beneath their specific differences, some generic resemblance to ASL. (p. 113)

Although it is no doubt interesting that exposure to English in signs, rather than facilitating English-like signing, fosters instead the development of ASL features and grammatical processes, the disparity in linguistic competence that emerges when one compares the development of English and ASL underscores the disservice that has been done to Deaf students over the years. In Livingston

(1983), I hypothesized five stages of ASL and English development in a study of six Deaf children of hearing parents exposed to Signed English by their teachers over a period of one and a half years. At each stage of development, but even more so at later stages, ASL afforded the students a decided advantage in expressing their intentions than did Signed English. This was true primarily due to the way the students used features of ASL grammar and, in particular, in the way they capitalized on the use of space through their body movement, eye gaze, indexing, and use of left and right hands. Coordination of these features at later stages of development allowed students to express their complex understandings in ways that Signed English could not.

It should not be surprising, then, that Deaf students understand ASL better than they do Signed English. If Deaf adults, who (for the most part) are more competent in English than Deaf children are, find it difficult to process Signed English, wouldn't Deaf children who are just in the process of learning language have even more difficulty understanding it? In addition, if children are forfeiting English structures in favor of ASL structures with which to communicate, it stands to reason that ASL would be more easily understood. In Livingston (1986), I reported on an informal study that asked ten Deaf children of hearing parents to demonstrate the meaning of a series of sentences by correctly manipulating dollhouse people and furniture. Almost consistently, both older and younger children understood in ASL, but not in Signed English, sentences that conveyed spatial relationships and were long and syntactically complex. Short and less complex sentences and sentences with predictable meanings were understood in Signed English. For the most part, then, when more meaning was being conveyed, Signed English could not fit the bill.

Similar results were obtained with older students in the context of a different, more difficult task. In Livingston, Singer, and Abramson (1994), forty-three Deaf college students watched first a ten-minute narrative and then a ten-minute lecture either through ASL interpretation or transliteration. Transliteration is a form of interpretation that maintains English word order. It draws signs in form and function from both English and ASL lexicons, as well as (in varying degrees) linguistic features (e.g., setting up locations in space) from ASL. Transliteration, however, is primarily English-based interpretation. Students were asked questions based on story and lecture content; the number of questions answered correctly was considered evidence of understanding. Students who received the presentations in ASL understood significantly more than students who received the presentations through transliteration. ASL interpretation was particularly more effective for the lecture presentation, as well as for questions that were long and syntactically complex. In addition, students with fewer years of college, as well as students judged to be less communicatively competent and less knowledgeable about the topic of the lecture, did significantly better with ASL interpretation than transliteration. The most intriguing result of this study, however, was that students judged to be English-sign dominant did significantly better with the ASL-interpreted lecture; their scores approached significance for the ASL-interpreted narrative.

ASL was clearly the kind of signing that provided the students in this study with more understanding. The fact that those students who were English-sign dominant understood far more via ASL than transliteration must mean that the linguistic features of ASL combined with the specific ways in which the presentations were interpreted (see Chap. 2, p. 33–36) are crucially needed to convey meaning—especially more complex meaning—visually and gesturally.

Yet despite the evidence against the use of Signed English, the lingering fear among most hearing teachers of Deaf students (and even more so among hearing parents of Deaf children) is that by not using it, Deaf students will never learn English. The truth of the matter is, however, that no Deaf person who knows English credits their knowledge of English to Signed English, nor do most Deaf people even feel comfortable using it (Livingston 1986). It is a system of signing that does not fit the meaning-making and meaning-sharing needs of a visual/gestural modality and, as such, conveys only gists or partial understandings of information that Deaf students are entitled to in full.

Some teachers have told me that they feel guilty even thinking about using ASL. Although I have never fallen totally in that camp, I must admit that when I first entered teaching, I too wondered how Deaf students were ever to learn English if they did not see it in sign form. I, along with many of my colleagues, embraced and staunchly supported the philosophy of Total Communication with a vengeance. I became "Sign Language Coordinator" and the primary architect of courses of study for parents and teachers, as well as the author of a two hundred-some-odd-page Signed English manual. Using signs to code English was revolutionary thinking—a far cry from the oralist tradition, whereby students were taught to listen (as best they could) and lipread to eventually speak English. It was a breath of fresh air.

But after several years of using Signed English, subtle signs of disillusionment started surfacing. We saw that our students' use of ASL far outstripped their English-sign abilities, and there were countless times when we needed to seek out a Deaf staff member to interpret what students were saying. How, in good faith, were we supposed to teach students we could not understand? We also couldn't help but compare the kind of communication that transpired between students and Deaf staff members and between students and hearing teachers. The former was spirited and substantive; the latter plodding, cursory, and replete with requests for repeats of what was said. We also never let on how often we would start out using Signed English and end by rephrasing our message in more understandable ASL-like ways, taking cues from the perplexed looks on our students' faces. What did this say about the quality of our teaching?

Perhaps most devastating was our recognition that reading and writing abilities showed little if any signs of improvement. Wasn't the promise of better readers and writers part and parcel of the rationale for Total Communication? Weren't students supposedly to read and write better by seeing visual English?

These questions did not sit well with me and their summative impact made me very ashamed. How could I justify calling myself a teacher knowing that the language I used to teach my students mitigated against the development of their minds? In my evolution as a teacher, this was the realization that forever changed me.

To the teachers who feel guilty about using ASL, I can only say that what they should feel guilty about is perpetuating a system that purposefully conveys only the simplest of meanings to Deaf students—a system that bypasses intellectual challenge in favor of ideas whose words teachers know how to sign. This is the kind of "talking down" that Darlene Shoemake refers to in her article in the *Silent News*—when in fact what they need most are complete understandings that they can sink their teeth into and thereby use to develop their minds. Yet ASL is still officially recognized as the language of instruction in only a handful of schools for Deaf students; many schools view its use only as a stopgap measure—as an "intervention strategy."

> The intervention agent [a teacher or language specialist] must first analyze a discourse situation to determine the need to use ASL. If ASL is necessary, the agent then uses ASL for a length of time dictated by the initial discourse factors that suggested its use. After this intervention period, the agent then switches back to using an English-based sign code. (Stewart 1991, 357)

This clinical approach to language acquisition views the use of ASL as merely an antidote to ineffective communication—a treatment to indulge in, and not for very long—once meaning has already broken down. Stewart goes on to explain that only communication "where a premium is placed on comprehension of concepts (e.g., science, social studies)" (p. 359) might be the appropriate contexts for the use of ASL. Isn't communication all about understanding concepts? What does this imply about concepts in the language arts and math, or is the premium on comprehension not as high in those areas?

It is time to stop feeding Deaf students pablum and instead to provide them with a real language that has the potential of offering them the eight thousand words, but more importantly the concomitant understandings as expressed by those words, that hearing students swallow up effortlessly even before they enter first grade (Ohanian and Vollmer 1989). Signed English just cannot make Deaf students that smart.

Applying Traditional Principles and Practices of Bilingual Education and Teaching English as a Second Language

In the literature of the field over the past several years, there have been recommendations to apply the principles of bilingual education and/or teaching English as a second language to the education of Deaf students. As representative examples, the National Association of the Deaf published a position paper on ASL and bilingual education stating that:

> (a) American Sign Language must be the primary language of instruction for academic subjects [and]
>
> (b) Instruction in English as the national language shall occur in parallel, based on pedagogical and linguistic principles used in bilingual/multilingual educational programs for other languages. ("ASL Position Paper Approved by NAD" 1994)

In addition, Johnson, Liddell, and Erting (1989) asserted that "ASL should be the first language of Deaf children, that English should be taught according to the principles of teaching English as a second language (ESL) and that the ultimate goal of the system is well-educated, bilingual [in the use of ASL and written English] children" (p. 15).

Although few would argue with Johnson, Liddell, and Erting's stated goal,—and it is certainly not the intention of this book to argue against Deaf students becoming bilingual—it is the means to achieving that goal—the principles and practices inherent in Bi-Bi (bilingual-bicultural) curricula—that need to be rethought.

But first, what is bilingual education and what are some traditional principles of teaching ESL? According to Carrasquillo (1990):

> The United States government defines bilingual education as instruction using the native language and culture as a basis for learning subjects until English skills have been sufficiently developed. . . .The primary objective of bilingual education is to facilitate students' acquisition of academic concepts. . .through the language students know best and to reinforce this information through the second language. (pp. 10-11)

Students typically remain in bilingual programs for two to three years and then exit into mainstream classrooms where they must learn in English only. This is known as the *transitional model,* wherein students are gradually weaned away from learning in their native language to learning exclusively in English. The assumption in bilingual education is that the understandings taught in one language will transfer to English. "If you teach concepts in one language, they do not need to be retaught (at least completely) in the other language" (Hakuta 1986, 218).

Methodologies used in bilingual classrooms vary widely. Hakuta (1986) describes one type of bilingual education program in broad outline:

> In the mornings, students from the same first-language group received instruction in that language in language arts and other subjects. In the afternoons, they switched over to their second language. At midday, the two groups were encouraged to mix at lunch and in programs in art, music, and physical education. During the midday lunch break the English and Spanish counterpart teachers exchanged information on the students' progress and coordinated instruction, so that the afternoon activities in the second language could extend and reinforce the morning lessons. (pp. 195-196)

In the Case Studies in Bilingual Education Project, developed in 1980 by the California State Department of Education, instruction in English is gradually phased in over four years. In Phases I and II, Spanish is the medium of instruction in language arts and social studies; at Phase II, children begin to receive instruction in math and science in English but in a "sheltered" way—"teachers change their speech register by slowing down; limiting their vocabulary and sentence length; repeating, emphasizing, and explaining key concepts" (Crawford 1991, 132). Some instruction in English language arts is offered in Phase III, and social studies starts to be taught in a sheltered way. Math and science are taught in mainstream classrooms. By Phase IV, somewhere around the fourth grade, the transition to instruction in English is complete except that classes in language arts continue in Spanish as a language maintenance feature of the model (Crawford 1991).

Often housed within bilingual programs are ESL classes, or separate classes for learning English. Traditionally, ESL teachers view themselves as strictly English-language teachers whose job is to teach English as a separate subject area or body of information. Students practice "survival language" and participate in simple, structured conversations, as well as various language activities geared to emphasize language functions (e.g., apologies and requests) or specific grammatical constructions. Speaking and listening are emphasized with little attention given to reading or writing during initial stages of instruction.

Although specific methodologies used by ESL teachers vary among school districts and are sometimes set by school administrations, teaching practices have traditionally (and still may) run the gamut from grammar-based *contrastive analysis* or *grammar translation* approaches, where students compare the structure of their native language with that of the language they are learning to pinpoint differences; to the *audiolingual approach,* where "language learning is seen as basically a mechanical system of habit formation [via mimicry and choral response], strengthened by reinforcement of the correct response; . . .and as such learned only by inducing students to 'behave'" (Paulston 1980, 300) by producing correct oral, grammatically sequenced pattern drills; to more *cognitive approaches,* which stress internalization of grammatical rules through intense listening to language that is preselected to call attention to specific grammatical constructions (Davidson 1980).

A considerable number of problems are inherent in applying the tenets of bilingual education, as well as the traditional ESL principles and methodologies discussed previously, to the education of Deaf students. First and most important, when Deaf students acquire communicative competence in both ASL and English, ASL will still be the language that best fits the constraints of the visual/gestural modalities both expressively and receptively—especially for more complex language. Therefore, even after knowledge of English has been sufficiently developed and becomes part of a student's sign competence, English in signs should not replace ASL as the language of instruction. There should not be exiting out of ASL classes into mainstream classes where only English is used. The transitional model as used in the field of bilingual education, then, has no place in the education of Deaf students.

Second, many bilingual programs compartmentalize instruction into times for majority and minority language use. But when ASL is the primary language used in schools for Deaf students, it is used throughout the day in all subject areas. English is used and learned when it is needed—when Deaf students read, write, and, for those with the requisite ability, lipread and speak. ASL, however, is not excluded during reading and writing times—it is, in fact, essential to their learning (see Chapters 3 and 4).

Third, traditional ESL approaches mistakenly view English as an amassment of grammatical parts that need to be contrasted with corresponding grammatical parts of a student's native language. These linguistic comparisons, it is thought, will make students aware of differences between the two languages. As such, English is learned for the sake of learning English grammatical structures with no real "beef" attached to its structural bones. In one program experimenting with the use of traditional ESL methodologies to teach Signed English to Deaf students, stories—each focusing on separate aspects of grammatical constructions or "themes" that differed markedly between ASL and English—were first presented in ASL and then

> in a strict manual version of English. . . .Children are [then] encouraged to look for differences in the two versions, with the teacher guiding them toward those that pertain to the theme of that particular unit. . .the goal is to introduce English and to show some of the ways in which it differs from ASL with a view to stimulating a metalinguistic awareness in the learners. (Strong 1988, 122)

Contrastive analysis methodologies such as these put grammatical constructions at center stage—at the heart of learning. Very few students, both young and old (but especially young), are intensely interested in learning the differences in ways languages are structured—except perhaps students of linguistics. By the time the story is signed for the second time, most students probably had already discovered what the story was about; I am left wondering how much they really paid attention to a comparative explanation about the bones, and if they did, to what avail. Learning how ASL is different from English will not be of much help in using or understanding either, just as "listening" to how riding a bike differs from rollerblading will not be of much help in either biking or blading.

Grammar-translation methodologies also have become popular in teaching writing to Deaf students. Teachers require students to first sign a story, assist them in glossing the signs and nonmanual features in English, and then proceed to show them how specific linguistic features incorporated in the signs and nonmanuals can be rendered in written English (Miller-Nomeland and French 1994; Togioka, Wolf, and Culbreath 1994). This tedious, unnecessary, and methodologically misconceived process presumes that English will be learned by noting how its bits and pieces differ or are similar to those that form the structural glue of ASL. It is using ASL to teach the written structure of English—using a "first" language to teach a "second"—the trap into which many advocates of bilingual education for Deaf students unfortunately have fallen; they believe this will help Deaf students learn written English. What Deaf students must learn, however, is how meaning—one's intent—is actualized in written English *directly and wholly*. Rather than needing to know the similarities and differences in the grammatical ways two languages express the same intent, students need to see how, when writing, their meaning is realized in print and, conversely, when reading, what print means. English is learned by learning how written English works, not by learning how written English differs from ASL.

The stumbling block for teachers is thinking that students learning to write need to code switch from ASL to written English (language to language) and that students learning to read need to code switch from written English to ASL (language to language)—when instead what must be learned is how, for writing, to formulate their intentions through the use of written English (meaning to language) directly and, for reading, to formulate meaning through the reading of written English (language to meaning) directly.

Said differently, Deaf students need to do writing through English and reading through English. But, without a doubt, ASL interpretation needs to be recruited to make written English meaningful; in Chapters 3, 4, and 5, I offer ways in which this might transpire. It is unfortunate that grammar translation or contrastive analysis—stale ESL teaching methodologies—are being promoted as ways to educate Deaf students (Mahshie 1995). Teachers would fare much better taking courses in the teaching of writing and reading rather than those that compare the grammar of ASL and of English.

Traditional ESL methodologies are also grounded in the notion that speaking and listening, as more primary or first-developing language processes in first-language learners, should be taught before reading and writing. Many ESL programs sequence their courses according to language mode, and require speaking and listening classes prior to reading and writing classes. This thinking has led linguists and educators of Deaf students to strongly advocate that ASL be acquired prior to the learning of reading and writing (Johnson, Liddell, and Erting 1989)—even to delay the teaching of reading and writing until the fourth year of schooling (Paul 1990). But to wait for an "oral" language to develop before written language is introduced to students who are ready to read and write is to artificially sequence language processes that work best in tandem. "Oral and written language systems are structurally related, but one is not an alternative symbolic rendition of the other.

Moreover, written-language learning need not wait for oral-language acquisition" (Edelsky 1986; Harste et al. 1984; Hudelson 1984 as cited in Edelsky et al. 1991, 59). Consider Svartholm's (1993) thoughts on the teaching of writing:

> "Learning by writing" must be preceded by some other kind of linguistic input; linguistic output must be preceded by comprehensible input. . . .It ought to be reflected in the proportion of time given the two activities of "reading" and "writing." The former has the right of precedence and ought to be totally dominant in the first few years. (313-314)

To think that children should not write during the first few years of school overlooks how reading and writing influence each other. It is true that ideas from books commonly appear in the writing of Deaf children in the early grades, but it is just as true that Deaf children encouraged to write early on, catch on quickly in their reading to word spacing, big and small letters, line navigation, and the vocabulary they have used in their writing. Good readers make good writers; likewise, good writers make good readers.

Finally, the reason behind thinking that principles and practices from the fields of bilingual education and ESL are appropriate for the education of Deaf students stems from viewing Deaf students as ESL students. *Deaf students are not ESL students.* The majority do not have a true first language upon entrance into school as do most ESL students. ESL students typically focus on learning one additional language whereas Deaf students must learn two.

If, then, the view that most Deaf students are ESL students is ill-conceived, and if traditional tenets and methodologies from the fields of bilingual education and ESL do not fit the bill for Deaf students, to what theoretical framework do we turn? As I stated at the outset of this chapter, it is my belief that Deaf students are, first and foremost, students who learn much the way all humans learn regardless of their hearing or language status. Educational practice that best accommodates this belief stems from a particular theoretical stance on the nature of language and learning.

Principles and Practices Need to Be Meaning-Driven and Reciprocal

Most of my thinking is drawn from uncommonsense (Mayher 1990) and whole language (Edelsky, Altwerger, and Flores 1991) theories of how hearing students learn. Both theories are similar and are based on principles of first-language acquisition, which, according to the theorists, serve as underlying principles of all learning.

Uncommonsense theory, much like whole language theory, supports the view that first-language acquisition and learning in general are tacit, holistic, and top-down processes.

> Whenever analytically independent bits of knowledge and skill are acquired, they are mastered in the context of a meaning-making task [understandable/relevant/personally meaningful] and rooted in experience. In that sense, they are acquired in passing, on the way to doing something else which has a meaningful integrity for the learner. (Mayher 1990, 104)

In uncommonsense/whole language theory, there is no breaking down of what is to be learned into subparts and skills with the hope that it will somehow, sometime evolve into wholes. Wholes are different from the sums of their parts because they comprise "the simultaneous interaction of all these aspects of meaning. . . .'basics' are not separable atomic skills but are integral to and inseparable from the overall meanings being constructed" (p. 87).

> In a whole language perspective, it is not just oral language that counts as language. Oral language, written language, sign language—each of these is a system of linguistic conventions for creating meanings. . . . none is a secondary representation of the other. It means that *whatever* is language is learned like language and acts like language. (Edelsky, Altwerger, and Flores 1991, 9)

Reading, writing, and even subject-area knowledge, then, as language, are learned best not as ordered processes but in parallel. Rather than firstness or secondness in their learning, there is interdependence and reciprocity.

These few theoretical beliefs—the vital importance of whole, meaning-based, contextualized learning and the interdependence of knowledge, "oral," and written language—undergirds most of this book. Such beliefs are actualized in uncommonsense and holistic classrooms by teachers who view acquiring and sharing understandings as the key reasons students come to school. Rather than to learn their "ABC's," students come to school to learn about birds and dinosaurs; in acquiring bird and dinosaur understandings, they concomitantly acquire their ABC's. In such schools, teachers and students construct understandings, in part, through free and unstructured "talk" about topics of interest to the students. The goal of such talk is for students to discover meaning—the nitty-gritty whys and wherefores inherent in the different disciplines that constitute a school's curriculum. These understandings drive the curriculum, and language is used in their service. As students come to know, they evolve the language to show that they know and, in so doing, effect greater abilities to know and say even more.

Talk alone, however, will not be effective enough. Talk embedded in rich, supportive contexts more likely will do the trick. Uncommonsense and whole language teachers know what rich, supportive contexts are: the hands-on experiences, the presentations that include pictures and media, the dramatizations and computer simulations that embody the understandings to be learned. Language in such contexts serves to represent meanings already partially digested through the feel and image of prior experience. As new understandings are intertwined with students' existing repositories of meaning, they are, at some point, "recycled" and appear in students' language. Such new ways of thinking, as expressed in language, are essentially what teachers refer to when they talk about students who have a command of language. They are the students who have something to say.

Uncommonsense and whole language teachers also recognize the role that reading stories and nonfiction books plays in fostering understanding. Either read to or guided in their own reading, students come away knowing more. Stories pull students into different times and places, offering them opportunities to imagine and thereby come to internalize firsthand-like experiences. If they read several books on the same topic, they can easily become young experts. Encounters with books that students understand and enjoy make them smarter, as evidenced by a larger, more precise vocabulary and more complex ideas as expressed through more complex, book-like language. "Exposure to the more complex language available from reading [as well as to the concomitant complex ideas] does seem to go hand in hand with increased knowledge of the language" (Chomsky 1980, p. 229).

In schools that embrace the making and sharing of understandings as the reason why students come to school, writing is viewed as the means by which students share what they know, or what they are coming to terms with knowing, in written English. Rather than learning English for the sake of learning the principles of English language formation, knowing English is viewed as the means by which competence in expressing one's intentions in writing is achieved. We write to convey what we know and think, as well as to find out what we are thinking for ourselves in more private kinds of writing. And just as reading and oral language are inextricably interdependent, so are reading, oral language, and writing. Talking and reading—ways of making and sharing understandings—have profound effects on one's ability to write. They are the grist for our writing mills. An incredible amount of talking and reading took place years before this book was written and, during the writing, many of its ideas became even clearer to me as I struggled to elaborate and order them coherently for my potential readers. It was the grappling with ways of best presenting what I know, writing a little each day over an extended period, that simultaneously created new insights, as well as a more experienced writer.

You may be thinking that these meaning-based, reciprocal ways of coming to know cannot possibly happen with Deaf students because they "don't have language" and that language must be known before understandings can be acquired. This "common-sense" assumption has unfortunately dominated the field for decades and obviated the notion that without understandings, language will not develop. The more students understand—the more students are provided supportive contexts within which to use language, reading, and writing—the more their language systems will find ways of expressing such understandings. Just as hearing students in uncommmonsense and holistic classrooms enrich their language through reciprocal relationships among language, reading, and writing, so will Deaf students. The more Deaf students know, regardless of the fact that this knowledge was created through the use of ASL, the more they bring to and, therefore, are able to use to comprehend their reading and to create their writing. The more Deaf students learn through their reading and writing, the more ideas get recycled back into their use of ASL. Languages, then, transfer at a cognitive, intellectual level—each influencing and enriching the other. There are additional benefits of reading (and writing) as well.

> The strong relationship between reading and language development, whether oral, written, or signed, is usually interpreted as causal. It is argued that development in a particular language influences the development of reading. However, it is equally feasible to conclude from correlational data that proficiency in reading facilitates [English] language development. A more appropriate working hypothesis might be that the relationship between language and reading is bidirectional. (Limbrick, McNaughton, and Clay 1992, 309)

When Deaf students become readers and writers, they come to internalize or know not only the content of what they read and write, but also the form of English used to express that content. "According to whole language research, people can learn vocabulary, syntax, and stylistic conventions directly through written language" (Edelsky, 1986; Harste et al. 1984; Hudelson 1984 as cited in Edelsky et al. 1991, p. 59). Bidirectionally, or reciprocally, over time, this knowledge of form and content will impact their signing competencies, affording students more English-like ways of signing, if they so choose. As executed by Deaf bilinguals, contact signing without voice—which "uniquely combines ASL and ASL-like lexical items in a reduced English syntactic system" (Lucas 1989, 32)—is a direct outgrowth of competencies developed through meaningful exposure to reading and writing. As byproducts of learning how to read and write, Deaf students will have the option of conveying their understandings using either ASL or more English-based signing, depending on the situation and audience with whom they are conversing.   This, then, is how they will become true bilinguals.

In *Educating Deaf Students Bilingually*, Mahshie (1995) reports of much the same thinking by teachers of Deaf students in Denmark.

> As the students became confident in their skills in reading Danish, they also became increasingly skilled at using "signed Danish," even though this was not how they were addressed growing up. . . .[This] increasing ability to produce signs in Danish word order is based on knowledge of the language through high levels of literacy, rather than high levels of literacy being brought about by using signed Danish. (129)

I have argued that the conception of Deaf students as being vastly different from hearing students is one reason why the education of Deaf students has not been as effective as it could have been. I suggest that a model of educational theory and practice be drawn from uncommonsense and whole language teachers who squarely place meaning-making and meaning-sharing at the heart of their teaching. Within the past several years, this thinking has also surfaced among some ESL educators who now support the idea that language-learning processes, including the development of reading and writing, are essentially the same for both first- and second-language learners, and that instructional activities typically found in meaning-centered mainstream classrooms are appropriate for all students (Boyle and Peregoy 1990; Cummins 1994; Genesee 1994; Hudelson 1994). Embedded in this thinking is recognition that language is learned when the focus of instruction is not on language but on achieving subject-area understandings, and that learning a second language in school is not exclusively for the sake of learning the language but rather as the means to achieve academic success. Thus, ESL researchers such as Cummins advocate the integration of language teaching and the teaching of academic content, which will simultaneously promote language and content mastery. Most important, he states that:

> The modifications to the instructional program required to integrate language and content in a manner appropriate for students do *not* entail a dilution in the conceptual or academic content of the

instruction, but rather require the adoption of instructional strategies that take account of students' academic background and ensure comprehension of the material being presented. (42-43)

Rather than adapting existing materials or creating special materials to match low-level English competencies (much like many teachers of Deaf students unfortunately spend much of their time doing), Cummins advocates keeping the content the same but changing instructional approaches to assist students in understanding the message. Such approaches are taken directly from meaning-centered classrooms and include peer tutoring, cooperative learning, and project-oriented activities that, according to Cummins, are effective for both academic and linguistic development.

Regardless of their language or hearing status, then, students learn in much the same ways. Differences arise only in the language(s) used, the degree to which contexts need to be facilitative and, perhaps, the time required to digest understandings that might come more quickly for those students who have been immersed in the language of instruction, reading, and writing as their first language. These differences can be easily accommodated when more appropriate language learning theories and educational practices are understood and implemented. In the following chapters, we look at the ways it has been and then at suggestions for the ways it might be.

Chapter Two

Developing Competency
in American Sign Language

The Non-teaching of Language

I cringe when I hear the words *language curriculum* used to refer to
a course of first-language study for Deaf students. To me it means
teaching language as if it were science or math or social
studies—teaching a body of knowledge that can be categorized,
ordered, and presented in some agreed-upon way based on levels of
complexity. It rings of calling students' attention to "important
facts" and their subsequent regurgitation. It leads one to believe that
the structures of a first language are just as teachable as how seeds
become plants, how to multiply fractions, or Marco Polo's route to
the Far East.

Here are some excerpts from a typical Signed English language
curriculum for Deaf students. In a section called "The Language
Learning Environment," the author explains how mothers of young
hearing children speak simply and clearly to them, calling their
attention to regularities in the language. The author then quotes
Streng, Kretchmer, and Kretchmer (1978), who say, "If normally
hearing children learn language in an environment controlled and
focused by their mothers, it seems reasonable that hearing-impaired
children too could benefit from such systematic linguistic exposure" (p. 48). This conjecture establishes the theoretical underpinning of the curriculum, which calls for the use of the following basic
sentence patterns throughout the school day:

NP + (AUX) + Vi   Juan laughed.
                         They can come.

NP + (AUX) + Vt + NP	The boys played football.
	The nice girl will eat her lunch.
NP + (AUX) + be + NP	Your mother is a nurse.
NP + (AUX) + LV + NP	Maria has become a bus driver.
NP + (AUX) + be + ADJ	She was very sweet.
NP + (AUX) + LV + ADJ	Mabel does seem ill.
NP + (AUX) + be + ADV	Tony is here.
	The class will be next Thursday.

These patterns, according to the author, "provide the child with the means to express the increasingly complex concepts that are developed as the child matures" (p. 22). She adds that there are transformations that can be used as children progress through the last level that form more complex sentences out of the basic pattern: sentences that express conjunction and subordination, as well as complementation. But the basic patterns are primarily those that teachers are encouraged to emphasize (i.e., talk/sign in) when conversing with their students, as well as the patterns they are told to expect back from their students in everyday conversation in order for them to meet their "behavioral objectives" in language. "For example, if a teacher wants to facilitate a child's acquisition of linguistic structures which express attribution, activities will be planned in which adjectives can be used frequently in short, simple sentences. . .which provide frequent opportunities for the child to use adjectives" (p. 24). "The curriculum is then used to determine the next set of structures in the developmental sequence that should be the focus of the language learning environment" (p. 25).

This, then, is language as content—specific language information is created, systematized in a simple to complex way, taught, and asked for back. It is neat and pleasing to some administrators and teachers, but it is, unfortunately, dead wrong. Such systemization "may be fine for imparting information and teaching content (math, science, etc.), but language skills *lack* an essential content, do *not* consist of information, and resist piecemeal teaching" (Mellon 1981, 58). Learning and using a first language are acts as unconscious as digesting food, learning how to walk, and getting taller; as contradictory as this may appear, in order for students to learn a first language, teachers must stop teaching it.

This notion has been perhaps the hardest for teachers of Deaf students to understand because it presupposes a working knowledge of how children think and learn in general, as well as some basic understandings about the nature of language and its acquisition. Piaget (1977) views children's thinking and learning as primarily self-directed, active processes that work best when children are physically engaged and interacting with their environment.

Learning occurs when children note both similarities and differences with existing understandings, then construct new mental categories or concepts to let in this different or new information. This view of conceptual development places children at the center of their own learning: What children learn is essentially what they come to know on their own as a result of their attention to new input that demands change in existing ways of understanding and thereby more enriched ways of looking at their environment.

It is within an environment such as this, where children are actively creating new understandings, that language can be acquired, if language is being used to assist children in their knowledge creation. This is a far cry from the purposeful teaching of language for the sake of having children learn language. Instead, this is the use of language that assists the child in creating understandings about concurrent activities through meaningful conversations that focus on making and exchanging ideas, as opposed to an emphasis on linguistic structures.

In the former environment, teachers are forced to think and converse in prescribed structures because the topic of the day's language lesson is a particular structure. In the latter environment, for example, teachers are thinking and conversing about seeds taking root, in ways they deem appropriate, because that is the topic of the day's science lesson. In such an environment, language is at the service of meaning. There are no language lessons; only meaning to be made and shared. And as meaning is made and shared, linguistic structures are tacitly acquired.

To buy into this notion, some background understanding into the nature of language and how it is acquired must be discussed. For this, we turn to the work of Noam Chomsky who, since the 1950s, has championed the theory of generative linguistics. A major tenet of the theory holds that the rules of language use are as unconscious to the users as the development of the embryo is to the fetus. In short, we are oblivious to how we say what we say. In fact, when we become conscious of the ways in which we use our language, of how we make our sentences, our words and, concomitantly, our thoughts do not emerge as we intended. When our minds are on our points, our words will take us there in ways unbeknownst to us.

Another property of language is its creativity. There is no book of ready-made sentences from which we choose those that are fitting for a particular context (except for perhaps greetings, idioms, and sayings). The majority of sentences that we speak and understand in a day are sentences that we, most likely, have never spoken or heard before; the ability to generate such sentences is one of the defining characteristics of being human.

There could be no better example of this than the talk of children that we find so endearing and, at times, downright hysterical. When my daughter was two years old, she adored mashed baked potatoes and got them with almost every meal. One day during the throes of toilet training, in her quest for privacy, she waved her hand at me and told me to "Go bake a potato." She never heard that sentence from me. She might have heard: "I'm going to bake you a potato now"; or "I'm going to make you a baked potato"; or even "I'm going to put a baked potato in the toaster oven." What she did was formulate her intention with the principles of language organization she had abstracted up until that point, constrained by the four or five words that comprised the typical length of her sentences. There can be no better testament to the creative nature of language than listening to the language of children.

There is ample evidence that Deaf children born to Deaf parents acquire ASL just as unconsciously and creatively (Klima and Bellugi 1979; McIntire 1992). However, regardless of this very fortunate advantage, these children still must endure the misguided approaches to language learning many schools for Deaf children abide by, as exemplified on pages 19–20. For such children, however, the ramifications of inappropriate pedagogy do less harm than for those children who arrive at school virtually languageless—Deaf children born to hearing parents who do not sign.

Conscious control and the spoon-feeding of syntactic rules defy existing knowledge about the nature of acquiring language. If it is known that acquiring language is more the work of the learner than the teacher, why do writers of language curricula insist on doing all the work—digesting adult language into bite-sized smidgens and spewing them out in an orderly way? If the process of first-language learning is an unconscious one on the part of the learner, why do writers of curricula abide by a very deliberate blueprint for language development, and profess to know the forms of language children need to use and when they need to use them? There is no way to know what aspects of language children are attending to at any given time simply because the process is unconscious. In addition, each child interprets his own world in very unique ways; what one child is zeroing in on might be the farthest thing from another child's mind.

Purposefully simplifying language to assist children in acquiring it is detrimental to the development of mind because it strips away the richness and wholeness of a system that all children need exposure to in order to learn. Conceptual development cannot thrive in impoverished linguistic environments. As active learners, children need opportunities to detect the commonalities in varied and complex language—to work with an overall view, to focus on what is intriguing them at a particular moment—which they cannot do if they are force-fed a steady diet of bland structures. As John Mayher (1990) states:

> The simplifications do serve to reduce the amount of input to the child, but in such a way as to rob her of the rich context necessary to fully interpret them, to connect them to her emerging cognitive and linguistic systems, and therefore to make them fully meaningful in any sense. Further, insofar as they are "deviant" forms, structures which do not conform to the system that the child is trying to learn, they may provide the bases for false rather than accurate hypotheses about the target language, and therefore slow down rather than enhance the process of learning it. Given the elusive and subtle properties of the language system revealed by generative linguistic analysis, and the fact that these properties are completely unknown to us as day-to-day language users, it seems unlikely on the face of it that we could provide relevantly simple and nondistorted input to language learners on the basis of our conception of the situation. (123)

The guiding principle of the language curriculum exemplified on pages 19–20 stems from the research on "motherese"—a label for what some researchers have called the kind of simplified speech that some mothers and caretakers use with children some of the time. This kind of talk avoids complex constructions, substitutes nouns for pronouns, and in general simplifies utterances by making them considerably shorter. Interestingly, it has been difficult for researchers to determine which, if any, of the changes in adult speech facilitates language acquisition. More to the point, Dale (1970) states outright that:

> The extent of simplification in maternal speech should not be overestimated. Every study that has compared maternal speech with the child's own language at the same time has found that the mother's speech is significantly more complex than the child's speech. Brown and Hanlon (1970) calculated that only 30 percent of the sentences heard by the child are simple, active, affirmative, declarative sentences. The remaining 70 percent are complex, passive, negatives, questions, fragments, and other forms. (145)

There seems to be little theoretical grounding, then, for the purposeful teaching of adult-simplified language. The "put this structure in; get this structure out" principle of language development that serves as the rationale for many language curricula used in schools for Deaf children also defies existing knowledge about the creative nature of language. As we have seen in the "Go bake a potato" example on page 22, children are far from little Xerox machines. Try as we might, there is no way of coaxing a child to say something that she hasn't yet discovered how to say on her own. Language patterns that are not in synch with the mental organization of a child will not be remembered because they cannot be assimilated into that child's existing neural framework and, therefore, remain meaningless to her.

In many schools for Deaf children it is not uncommon to see students memorizing phrases and sentences. It has even been suggested that teachers use intervention strategies such as "arranging environments" or "sabotaging routines" (Luetke-Stahlman 1993) so that children are forced to use language in ways that adults want them to. Insisting that these children copy language or speak on command as opposed to allowing them to create language in their own child-like ways shows little faith in the fact that Deaf children have the same language-acquiring brains as hearing children.

Although I never asked my daughter to repeat utterances that I modelled, I will admit that when she was acquiring language, I would catch myself correcting and recasting some of her sentences. I quickly stopped, however, when I realized that she found what I was doing irrelevant and rather nonsensical. It was as if she were thinking, "If you don't have something new and interesting to tell me, why are you talking?" After all, I was saying essentially the same things she was, but in an adult way. I also picked up on the fact that while I was recasting, she was somewhere else—both in a physical and a mental sense. I came to understand how form was just so inconsequential to her. She was looking for new discoveries; I was pushing correctness.

Yet in most schools for Deaf children it is unfortunately the case that because teachers have "language objectives" to teach and "intervention strategies" to "accelerate" the normal development of language, the kind of language that transpires is both vapid and stilted. However, at the same time it is rather comforting for those teachers whose Sign competence requires that they control the conversation and converse only in the simplest structures they can execute. The effect, sadly, is to retard rather than to accelerate. Teachers talk to their students for the sake of using language without a real purpose other than to have a particular structure stick. It is disheartening to note that some researchers are now suggesting that certain grammatical aspects of ASL should be formally taught to children learning it as a first language (Paul and Quigley 1994). Such thinking is quite common when language curricula dictate teaching language as content (e.g., teaching related verb-noun pairs in ASL). It will be unfortunate if ASL, a language so powerful in conveying meaning to Deaf students, becomes trapped in outdated views of language education.

But suppose language were viewed more as a vehicle for making and sharing information. How would this affect language acquisition? For one thing, there would be neither language curricula, language objectives, nor intervention strategies to accelerate language acquisition because our goal would be to make Deaf children more intelligent by assisting them in learning more about their world. Rather than focusing on language development, our curricula would focus on the development of mind through the use of language. Teachers would not have prescribed structures to "talk" in nor intervention strategies to orchestrate. Their major responsibility would be to provide the richest possible learning environment and plenty of opportunities for children to talk with them, older students, and each other.

This rich learning environment would include interrelated activities in math, science, social studies, and language arts, where children would naturally encounter information worth talking about; where learning experiences would be activity-based; where children would be presented with authentic problems to solve and opportunities to hear each other's thinking about possible solutions; and where selected activities would respect the developmental stage of individual learners. With understandings rather than language at the core of this new curriculum, children would make and share their new discoveries in language—learning language as a byproduct rather than a discipline unto itself.

How Shall We "Talk" with Deaf Students?
Teachers as Interpreters

In their teacher-training programs, prospective teachers of Deaf students have probably heard all too often the phrases, "Bathe Deaf students in language," or "Talk, talk, talk to Deaf children." Although these basic notions are important, they do not convey the idea that the kind of talk that must transpire needs to make an impact on students; talk that makes sense to them, talk that makes ideas understandable and therefore memorable. Of course, using ASL will facilitate understanding, but what I am referring to goes beyond the use of ASL: I am talking about the need for teachers to be interpreters for Deaf students.

I have always marveled at the way expert interpreters practice their art. In fact, to me, the difference between the experts and the "okay" interpreters is that the former are artists, the latter are practitioners. The difference is one of philosophy and not necessarily translation skill. (My category of "okay" presupposes the fact that skill is a given.) The artists feel free to create; the practitioners feel safer transliterating messages employing sign-for-word or phrase equivalences. Artists do what they feel will convey meaning; practitioners follow the path already laid out by the speaker. Artists think, "What does it take for me to understand a particular message and how best can I convey that via Sign?" Practitioners think, "What is the sign for that word or group of words?" The former considers where the audience is coming from and what is needed for that particular audience to understand a message; the latter translates the same sentence in the same way no matter who the audience. As stated by an artist, "My hands get tired, but not as much as my brain does" (Filichia, 1996, p. 21).

I hear rumblings that although this might be accurate within the field of interpreting, it doesn't apply to teachers. I must disagree. One of the major reasons why the education of Deaf students has been without great success is because, in addition to the fact that a natural language has not been used, the way that teachers attempt to communicate with their students is (in general) harmful to true understanding. Far too often, teachers talk to Deaf students as if they had the same number of years of experience with the way certain understandings are conveyed through language as they do. Words are exchanged for signs without regard for the fact that students do not share the same mental models (Johnson-Laird 1983) as adults.

Rather than trying to sign in ways that make connections between mental models, it is not uncommon for teachers to get wrapped up in adult wording, making their points far removed from students' social and cognitive perspectives. Thinking might run something to the effect that, "If I am signing it in ASL, then students will understand it." But what we say, especially to children, is often not understood the way we would like it to be. This is because our thoughts are often not directly encoded in our words or signs. What we mean to say is often behind our remarks and what we reveal in our words is essentially only the tip of the whole iceberg. "There is more going on than just the direct equivalence of expression and thought in the process of communication" (Mayher 1990, 143).

If teachers expect Deaf students to fully understand them, they need to become the kind of interpreters described as artists. This does not mean that they must possess a Certificate of Interpretation. It means they need to know what it takes to understand a particular idea and how to assist a particular audience in understanding it in the appropriate contexts that need to be created within which meaning can be made and shared. We explore how this might be done next.

Facilitating the Creation of Mental Images

Several years ago, the day before Christmas vacation, I dropped my daughter off at her kindergarten class. As I was leaving, I told Laura, a friend of hers, to have a good vacation. Laura followed me to the door and asked, "What's a vacation?"

Adults often take for granted what children know. There are times when I find myself asking my nine-year-old daughter if she knows what I mean after expressing a thought; it is rather sobering to see how often my intent evades her and needs to be said in other words. It is rarely the basic thought that is beyond her; rather, it is the language used to express it that is too "adult." Nor is it the language in a syntactic sense, as she has had a good command of embedded clauses, complement phrases, and the like for quite some time. It is more an issue of particular word choices and eclipsed, truncated meanings to which adults, who have lived longer and talked more than children have, subscribe. Our understandings, as expressed through our language, are compressed and layered as a result of our "rich constellation of conceptual and experiential connections" (Mayher 1990, 78). In a manner of speaking, when we talk with children, we need to do some idea "unpackaging."

I do not know if Laura's family ever took a vacation, but I imagine even if they had, it would not have helped Laura with her question. Laura was also not looking for a definition of the word vacation. If I had said, "It's a holiday; a recess; freedom from any activity," or even something more accessible perhaps, such as "a time to rest," I doubt it would have fit Laura's bill. She wanted to know how what I said affected her in her own very specific terms.

Being an intense kid-watcher over the past nine years with my own daughter has led me to the understanding that when she was really registering or connecting with a particular idea, a glazed, distanced kind of look and a momentary pause in her activity would overtake her. It was as if she was "seeing" what I was talking about in her own mind—a reading of an internal picture screen. This observation is far from being exclusively a maternal revelation; rather, it reflects the thinking of George Lakoff (1987), who claims that our understandings stem "from our imaginative projections of likenesses and contrasts based on our bodily experiences" (as cited in Mayher 1990, 160). And, as reiterated by Mark Johnson (1987):

> Imagination is central to human meaning and rationality for the simple reason that what we can experience and cognize as mean-

ingful, and how we reason about it, are both dependent upon
structures of imagination that make our experience what it is. . . .
The structures of imagination are part of what is shared when we
understand one another and are able to communicate within a
community. (172)

Understanding, then, would appear to be the ability of "listeners" to imagine or reconstruct a picture in their minds, based on
their perceptual experiences and conceptual systems, that is a
close enough approximation to the kind of understanding "speakers" intend to communicate. But how does one create images
through words so that listeners can do an appropriate "read" of
their picture screens?

When Laura asked me what a vacation was, I remember having
an instantaneous dialogue with myself about how best to create a
response, asking myself, "How can I assist Laura in re-creating what
she herself most likely does when she is not in school," which
means that I was working between what I assumed to know of her
world and the "time off" feature of the adult meaning of the word. I
replied, "You get to stay home and watch cartoons in your pajamas." I hoped to offer Laura the opportunity to create an image of a
familiar happening during the hours she is not at school and any
concomitant effect, such as the sights and smells of a leisurely
breakfast or the comfort of loose-fitting pajamas. She appeared over-
joyed at the thought—a rather tangible sign of understanding in this
particular case.

Are we then talking about relating what children already know
to what they are in the process of learning? Yes, but more than that.
The kind of language we choose to use to relate old and new experiences when we talk with students, Deaf or hearing, needs to
enable them to create mental images. Although there is a time and
place for descriptive phrases to make language come alive, I am
talking more about language that represents a student's particular
reality in visual terms—the kind of language that embraces the
everyday scenes of students' lives through example or approxima-
tions of these scenes through analogy. This kind of language is not
for students only—it works for the most learned among us as we
grapple with truly understanding the thoughts of another. "People
understand and internalize information through the vividness of
familiar and shared experiences" (Roy 1989, 248).

Consider a discussion I had one semester with my college-aged
Deaf students that centered on an understanding of the word *petition*. We had come across the word in Greenberg's (1970) novel *In
This Sign*, and my students were unable to recognize the word in
print but professed to know its meaning once its sign was shown

Delving deeper, however, it soon became apparent that most of the students had incomplete understanding of the term, as evidenced in Penny's response:

> Like for example, Girl Scout cookies. . .if you want to buy that so you sign your name and you get money. It's like supporting them.

Joe offered a more accurate but still not totally accurate explanation:

> I know. Something came up where I live. There's a Bath Avenue and there's a street and there's a red light so when a car is coming there's no light so a car coming could hit somebody and they complained about that over and over again so to have a petition to have traffic control they want to put a light or they want to bring it to court.

We used Joe's example as our jumping-off point, pointing out how he first explained that there was a problem that people wanted resolved and his subtle reference to authority in the form of a traffic-control agency or court. But real understanding happens when we strike an emotional, "close-to-home" chord (as Joe's example did for him); in this case, there could have been no more perfect example than the issue of the (at times) limited supply of interpreters at our college. Most of my students lived and breathed the problem several times during a semester and were very aware of the authorities to whom they would need to appeal—the Program Director, the Dean, and even the Chancellor. We talked about power in numbers and how it would be incumbent upon the petition-creators to gather signatures of both day and evening students along with their colleagues in Continuing Education. We planned what the petition would say, the most efficient way of collecting signatures, and how they would approach their classmates.

I feel fairly confident that an image was created in my students' minds about petitions and in Laura's mind about vacations because of the use of emotional connections and detailed information with which they were thoroughly familiar. Upon subsequent encounters with those words, they are bound to re-picture or re-create this personal meaning in their own unique ways because a record or pattern of understanding has already been formed. These, then, are examples of what I mean when I talk about teachers functioning as interpreters. It would not have been enough to talk about the terms in a distant, definitional way. The terms needed to be interpreted—personalized and made relevant in ways that students could "see" and "feel."

Being Explicit

> Before we had captioning on television my family and I would sit and watch a program or movie, and when the movie would stop for the

> commercials we would all take that time to speculate on the story and
> create what was happening and guess at what was going to happen
> next . . . . This was not just my family, but lots of Deaf families played
> this game. To be honest, now with captioning and seeing the dialogue
> I think that a lot of our stories were better. (Rutherford 1993, 82-83)

Television and movies aside, this very telling example reveals
only the tip of the speculation-and-guessing iceberg that those Deaf
people who choose to interact with the hearing world experience
during the course of their daily lives. Information gained from participation in conversation, overheard conversation, loudspeakers,
and radios evades them and, if reading is not a fluent skill, a lack of
general knowledge is the price they pay. "With this understanding
we can also appreciate the high value that is placed on information
by Deaf people. It is the person with information, not necessarily
the esoteric Ph.D., who is the more highly regarded" (p. 82). This is
the person who knows about the workings of the world as gleaned
from reading and/or conversation. Although it is undoubtedly true
that much of what we learn is learned through visual and perceptual means, as discussed previously, there is no denying the role that
language plays in explaining those things that cannot be understood
through visual and perceptual ways alone. "Try to explain the rise
and fall of the Communist republics without using a single word"
(Damasio and Damasio 1993, 54).

In a study of how much six Deaf children exposed to Signed
English for a year and a half (Livingston 1981) understood of the
story *Hansel and Gretel,* as told to them by their teachers in Signed
English, the explanatory power of language was made astonishing-
ly clear. The children, aged eight to sixteen, all born to hearing parents, were asked to retell the story using the picture book to guide
them. With limited exposure to an ineffective sign system for meaning-making, this turned out to be more a study of the deleterious
effects that inappropriate input and lack of language facility have on
understanding than a simple test of "listening" comprehension.
Parts of the story that were language-dependent (in other words, not
pictured) were almost entirely missed by all but two of the oldest
students. These parts included the following:

- the reason for the stepmother's plan to abandon Hansel
  and Gretel
- the reason for the breadcrumbs trail
- the effect of the birds eating the breadcrumbs trail
- Gretel's plan to throw the witch into the fire
- the witch's fatal error of believing that Gretel did not understand her order

With limited understanding of the real story, the students made up their own, which were fraught with misinterpretations, for example:

- After Gretel heard the stepmother's plan to leave her and Hansel in the forest, she started to cry. One of the students interpreted this to mean that she was a bad girl. Another thought it meant that she was hungry.
- After Hansel and Gretel's father left the children in the forest, I asked one of the students if she knew where he went. She replied, "To the ugly witch's house." Hansel and Gretel's father was pictured there at the conclusion of the story.
- The stepmother gave Gretel the basket with the bread so that Gretel could sprinkle crumbs on the grass.

Notice, however, that these individual interpretations were not without logic or imagination. There is nothing amiss with the underlying reasoning or imagining abilities as expressed in these examples. What is missing is story information with which to direct these reasoning abilities to the particular story line. Of interest is the kind of information housed in these missing language-dependent portions of the story. They express reasons for actions, plans (references to time), implications, and trickery—all abstract ways of using language that develop over time from meaningful exposure to and use of an accessible language. They reflect the power that language has to extend, inform, and specify our thinking.

It will not be stretching the point to say that these were most likely the aspects of the television movies that the Deaf person quoted on p. 30 missed as well—but for obviously different reasons than the children referred to in the *Hansel and Gretel* study. The movie-watcher, from a Deaf family and most likely bilingual, was not physically receiving language that he was perfectly capable of understanding. The children in the study, still in the process of acquiring full competence in language, were being exposed to a sign system of which they could make little sense. In the example of Penny, the college student who was only coming to terms with an understanding of the word petition (see p. 29), we see understanding based on partial features of the meaning of the word. She understood the idea that a petition requires signatures and that it is a statement of support, but it was the reason for its use that she hadn't yet digested, most likely because no one had explained it to her. These examples speak to the costly effect that inaccessible language, for whatever reason, has on one's ability to receive information; without information, there is little understanding and what understanding there is is often idiosyncratic.

How then does this relate to talking with Deaf students? Beyond the obvious need to talk with them in an accessible language there is the need to talk in ways that acknowledge the fact that they have been guessing about or have missed a lot of information in their lifetime. Add to this the fact that once past the *Hansel and Gretel* stage, both oral and written discourse becomes less forgiving; much of what is said and written is buried in the context of a particular oral or written text. For Deaf students in the process of acquiring competence in language, meaning that is between the lines only serves to further stymie them. The plain fact is, however, that much of what we say and read is replete with implicit messages. To understand a speaker's or writer's intent, we must be prepared to do a considerable amount of interpretation, as this example, adapted from the work of Roger Schank, illustrates:

> Mary saw the ice-cream truck coming down her street. She remembered her Christmas money and ran inside (Kendig 1983, 30).

Where in these two sentences is the following information?

> Mary is a girl
> Mary is outside.
> Mary wants ice cream.
> Mary got money as a Christmas gift.
> Mary is excited.
> Mary went to get money.

We understood the example sentences by making inferences—by calling upon our extensive knowledge of the world to supply unstated but implied information. These understandings lurk in our memories waiting to be summoned in ways that we are still trying to figure out. The Catch-22, though, is that if "interpreting language is. . .a process of. . .making meaning anew through reconstructing our own sense of [it] through the filter of our own experience" (Mayher 1990, 158), how helpful can these experiences or understandings be if they have not been appropriately and adequately linguistically represented? How possible would it be to form connections if memories are not in some way recorded in our minds? Without information to draw on that can assist us in interpreting the oral and written texts of our world, much understanding will allude us.

Remember also that in the educational arena, teachers (most of whom are hearing) and students do not interact using equivalent language systems, nor do they draw their experiences from similar cultures. My "buried message," then, is that communication between teachers and students has (at least) four strikes against it. These strikes stem from teachers who are without solid grounding in ASL, many still believing that the use of ASL is somehow harmful to the English-learning process; have limited understanding of the culture of Deaf people; unconsciously use language in ways where its meaning too often lies below the surface of what is actually said; and are unaware of the limited frames of reference some students bring to the communication setting. The scenario is bleak but not irreparable.

Competence in ASL and a firm grasp of the culture of the Deaf community notwithstanding, teachers must be able to penetrate the core of an idea and bring it to the surface in ways that make sense to students who have been denied an accessible language for too many years. As recently discerned in a study of the effectiveness of ASL interpretation versus transliteration (Livingston, Singer, and Abramson 1994), more effective communication with Deaf students necessitates making what is implicit in oral text explicit. In this study, more effective ASL interpretations, as judged by more accurate answers to questions posed about the content of a ten-minute narrative and a ten-minute lecture, were characterized by several strategies used either less frequently or not at all in other ASL interpretations of the same information from which students understood considerably less. The strategy that we called explicitness entailed further explanation that went beyond the given text to include its underlying message, as well as any background knowledge, further clarification, or affect necessary to understand the speaker's intent. Following are examples of explicitness from the study:

Text: So the person who asked me the questions was nice and friendly, but she had to ask me questions sometimes three or four times before her question would sink in and before I could think of a way to respond.

Interpretation: The woman asked me questions continuously and many times the same question, not because I was dizzy, *because I couldn't pay attention. I was nervous thinking and obsessing about my son and couldn't answer her.* She continued to ask me questions again and again.

The underlying reason why the narrator had difficulty responding to questions, which needed to be inferred from the story the students were watching, was overtly stated.

Text: . . . but in my head I knew I had to bring insurance cards to the hospital because I've had some experience with that before.

Interpretation: I knew I had to bring my insurance cards. Why? Because *I had to bring them to the hospital as proof that my insurance would pay for everything.*

Some background information about insurance cards, not included in the text, was provided here.

Text: This story occurred last summer and I teach summer school. And summer school ends on Thursday. So Thursday afternoons I drive out of New York City to spend some time with my family.

Interpretation: This story happened last summer. I'm a *college teacher* in summer school. What happens is on Thursday afternoons I finish. *I forget about my class here* and what do I do? I hang out with my family in a different place. *They're very special to me and I look forward to spending time with them.*

Note how this interpretation creates a certain feeling. The narrator forgets about his job concerns and looks forward to three full days with his family who are near and dear to him. Note also how the reason why summer school ends on Thursdays is directly stated—because the narrator is a college teacher.

Explicitness, then, serves to state the unstated. It can provide reason, background knowledge, affect, and clarification. By so doing, it ties together what might otherwise be disparate pieces of information for which connections within a particular text might not be made. Without such connections, we do not come to know. Explicitness provides the glue that language users assume "listeners" or readers bring to listening and reading. It assists in making sense of what might remain senseless to those who have not had mainstream language exposure and, in so doing, facilitates the creation of literate minds.

Other Interpretation Strategies

Drawing on the Livingston, Singer, and Abramson (1994) study, I discuss several other strategies used in the more successful ASL interpretations and direct the reader to the actual study for detailed examples. The strategies describe both linguistic manipulations of text that capitalized on the grammatical features of ASL and specific strategies that interpreters who were "allowed" to use ASL used to craft the language in ways they felt would enhance understanding for their audience. The work, then, of some of the more artistic interpreters (if you will) is summarized in the following paragraphs.

Successful interpretations included pronounced use of *Rhetorical Questions* found in the grammar of ASL. These questions were used in the narrative to delineate major episodes of the story and, in so doing, carried through the thread of the story line. In the lecture, they called attention to the main points as they arose.

Constructing conversation out of reported speech was achieved through the use of body shifts and eye gaze. Essentially, portions of both the narrative and the lecture became dialogues between people where interpreters would step into characters' roles and actually portray conversation, as opposed to only interpreting what the narrators were saying about the interactions. This strategy clearly pictured who was saying what to whom. We called it *Stepping Into Character.* Roy (1989) called this strategy "constructed dialogue" and has written about its effectiveness in lectures given by Deaf speakers and in classrooms with Deaf teachers.

To emphasize a particular point, the more successful interpretations repeated the idea using alternate signs or sign phrases. Through *Repetition with Alternate Signs or Sign Phrases,* a particular sign would be used and then immediately backed up with a synonym sign or phrase. Many times this form of repetition was used to convey the feeling of a particular character.

Top-scoring interpretations included asides, often indicated by a body shift, to bring the listener back to an earlier portion of the text to bridge a new idea with a former one. This served to tighten connections within the narrative. At times, the signs REMEMBER and RECENT pulled parts of the story closer together, offering students a more direct path to understanding. We called this strategy *Referring Back.*

Creating Contrast Through Negation worked this way: Interpreters would create opposite meanings of statements, negate what they had just signed, then end with the narrator's original meaning. An example is needed here:

Text: So hospitals being a business, I had to go to the business office to check in.

Interpretation: Hospitals are free. . .Nope. Hospitals are businesses and money is owed.

The contrast set up in this way helped to make the point about hospitals being a business more emphatic.

There were several instances of particularly effective sign choices—signs or sign phrases that encoded the narrator's meaning in an image-creating, gestural, or pictorial way. One such choice was the sign used to convey *insurance card*. The interpreter, by depicting the opening and closing of a book to represent a cardholder where an insurance card might be kept, departed from the citation form of the sign CARD, which outlines the square shape of charge cards, licenses, and the like. We referred to this strategy as *Visual Sign Choices.*

For the lecture presentation only, when the information being expressed was detailed, complex, and new to the students, two strategies appeared to help students create meaning. At the conclusion of a point developed over several sentences, two of the top-scoring interpretations employed the use of summary statements.

Interpreters gave brief synopses of the preceding information before moving on to the next related topic. *Summaries* helped the students understand the theme of the lecture by focusing their attention on the point being made.

Related to this was the strategy we called *Explaining Before Labelling*. Interpreters would interpret the specifics of a particular concept before giving the students a name for it. Although the lecturer stated the name of a new term and then defined it, the interpreter held off labelling until there was enough information to which to anchor the label. Like the strategy *Summaries*, this strategy offered explanation first and a newer, more abstract way of "saying" it second.

Top-scoring interpretations revealed several distinctive ways of framing comprehension questions for students. Much like the strategy described as *Referring Back*, interpreters would listen carefully to the question, then provide the segment of the text from which the question was drawn before framing the question—essentially hooking up the student to the context of the question. Replaying the scene just before asking the question served to bring the students into closer contact with the time and place to which the question referred. This strategy was called *Contextual Hook Up*. Some interpretations included asides directing the students as to what the question required them to do. For example, when the lecturer asked, "What would be a masculine gender characteristic?," the interpreter would interpret the question and then add, FOR EXAMPLE. For the question, "Which of the four agents of socialization do you think has the most effect on children and why?," the interpreter would add, PICK ONE THEN EXPLAIN WHY PT forward STRONG INFLUENCE. These *Question Aids* let the students know exactly what the question required them to do.

Although the roles of interpreters and teachers are distinct, they are not mutually exclusive. As seen from the prevous examples, the more successful interpretations for the students in the Livingston et al. study did, in fact, reflect a considerable amount of explaining and clarifying—teaching, if you will. I am advocating that teachers act more like artistic interpreters. Whether they are interpreting their own ideas or ideas inherent in other texts (as we will see in the next chapter), they must be effective with their language use—they must know how to talk with their students so that they have opportunities to become knowledgeable and imagine—so that they truly understand. In this way, they will be sought-after members in their communities.

Students Talking to Students

Glance around a schoolyard, school bus, lunchroom, or hallway at a school for Deaf or hearing students and you will undoubtedly see students busily engaged in "talk." This talk is spontaneous and, most often, about things of age-appropriate mutual interest. I have always been rather amazed at how much my daughter learns in these kinds of out-of-classroom contexts. Her talk at home typically refers to the happenstances of classmates gleaned from these very social arenas. In fact, that is all she talks about.

Bringing the animated and ongoing kind of talk that transpires in these social contexts into the confines of the classroom would considerably improve the chances of all children to learn language. Much like learning anything else, children must have wide and varied opportunities to do what it is they are trying to learn. They must practice it. A steady diet of "listening" will not do; students need to "do" language. Of course, there are times and places for teachers to talk to their students, but it is unfortunately true that most teachers talk too much and usurp precious time from students doing language. "While we can learn much about content. . .by listening to others, we do so much more effectively in a system that permits open give and take among equals" (Mayher 1990, 242). The opportunity to explore new ideas through conversations with our peers

> . . . is the fundamental process through which we further develop and enrich our language system. It's the way we learn new vocabulary, because we have the opportunity to hear it and produce it in a context where its appropriateness can be tested not in a punitive atmosphere, but in a mutually collaborative attempt to clarify meanings being made. It's the best opportunity we have for enriching the complexity of our syntactic repertoire by being in contexts where complex ideas naturally demand the use of complex structures by speakers and listeners. . . . (242)

In this section, I briefly focus on activities that capitalize on students talking to students outside of what is considered typical reading, writing, and content-area contexts. However, *please bear in mind* that the principles and activities set forth in this book are all sign-language-facilitating principles and activities because (as emphasized at the beginning of this chapter) the acquisition of sign language best transpires in all arenas where children are actively using language to explore and create new meaning. There is no one part of the day more than others that children learn sign language if schools foster meaningful learning via Sign throughout the day. *The learning of language is inseparable from the using of language in collaborative contexts where meaning is being made and shared.*

Play

Shawn Davies (1991) describes a study done by Ahlgren (1982) that brought Deaf nursery-school–aged children of Deaf and hearing parents together for "Saturday School" once a week for a year and a half. Three months after the end of the experiment, Ahlgren videotaped the children at play and asked a number of Deaf individuals to identify the children of Deaf parents based on their sign-language skills. The "judges" could not tell the difference between children with Deaf and hearing parents, which is typically easy to do with such young children. Considering the limited amount of time these children spent together, Ahlgren, as cited in Davies, states:

> . . . and it was obviously very easy for children to learn, and obvious that these children with hearing parents needed very little in the way of models. . . . My interpretation was, and still is, that the most important thing for these children was not to meet deaf adults, but to meet each other. It seems that is confirmed by many other observations, that children imitate the language of their peers, rather than of their parents. (6)

I do not think that Ahlgren means to downplay the important role Deaf adults play in the acquisition of sign language. In fact, Davies goes on to explain how in Sweden, where this study took place, special attention is given to placing Deaf adults in preschool-level classrooms. Instead, it is more the social nature of learning language through play that she appears to be emphasizing. As these children were becoming social, they were learning language; as they were learning language, they were becoming social. This kind of reciprocity works best in play contexts where children need to negotiate for turn-taking, colors of paint or crayons, front-row seats, and friends for the day. Such contexts provide opportunities to talk about clear, accessible, and highly valued topics of interest. Add to this context age-appropriate, ASL-competent playmates and the recipe for effortless language acquisition and content learning is just about complete.

Creative Drama

There is perhaps no better context within which language use can flourish than the context of creative drama, for it has been shown that children tend to be rather verbal during this time (Marshall 1961). Creative drama, supported by the use of props and costumes, offers students clear frameworks from which they can either stay within their immediate experience or jump off to express the creations of their imaginations. When students work together to orchestrate skits, they need to negotiate who they are, what they will be doing, and what objects will represent (Garvey 1977). Language use is most often tied to well-known contexts—ones created by the children themselves. These contexts provide the support needed for children to experiment with longer, more complex language use.

Creative drama also offers children exposure to the requirements of a good story. Teachers should roll up their sleeves, shed their cloaks of reserve, and feel free to model little vignettes, with appropriate props and costumes, for their students. A colleague and I used to have what we called "Showtime." We would perform daily "mini-shows" (no more than five minutes in length) wherein characters would get into predicaments that required some resolution—made up purely from our own imaginations. For children still at the beginning stages of language acquisition, these skits, primarily due to the support of props and costumes, were able to not only hold their attention but also to impact them so much so that they would stop us in the hallways weeks later to remind us of funny aspects of particular shows.

Once our opening show was completed, students divided into groups of four or five and were given a prop or costume to assist the flow of their own creative juices. With ample time to practice, and knowing that each group would be called upon to perform in front of a larger group of their peers, there was little difficulty in spurring students on in their work. Looking back at "Showtime," I recall some of the most engaging moments of my teaching career. It seemed that for one hour, neither teachers nor students could stop laughing or, sometimes, crying. Of that hour, I would estimate that each student had at least forty minutes to talk either with their peers or to a larger audience of teachers and peers.

For older students with more language experience, the dramatization of literature might be tried. "They are encouraged to think creatively and pretend to be their favorite characters" (Heinig 1992, vii) in circumstances and predicaments they have not read about. Children work in groups thinking of conversations particular characters could possibly have. As an example, Heinig suggests a possible conversation between Goldilocks and her mother concerning the whereabouts of Goldilocks all day. After some initial experience with this, students can try improvising familiar scenes but with a new slant, such as a different ending. Heinig (1992) suggests using folktales for incorporating drama into the classroom because they possess bold characters and fast-moving plots. Her book is composed of a wide variety of dramatic techniques that can be used with twenty well-known tales. Sign Media's (Burtonsville, Maryland) *High-*

Five Fables and Fairy Tales is a truly brilliant set of tales sign-told and dramatized on videotape that can get the creative juices of young students flowing—especially the tales that are first told the traditional way and then the way they would have been told if Deaf people had created them!

Children as Storytellers

Susan Rutherford (1993) describes the roots of a widely regarded storyteller among the Deaf community in California. Apparently, the storyteller's father, also Deaf, worked near the San Francisco Bay Bridge between 1933 and 1937 when it was being constructed and spent his lunch hour watching men erect it. A special sign communication developed among the workers who, although hearing, could not hear each other due to the racket caused by the construction.

> My father just loved it. It became quite a show. There was no TV in those days. So, my father filled the evenings with his stories of the day's events on the bridge. We could listen to him for hours on end. (81)

These are the children who become the very-much-in-demand storytellers at residential schools for Deaf children—the ones who stand next to the TV in the recreation room and create their own stories out of what is visually, but not linguistically, accessible. They are the children who become the storytelling role models for Deaf children who cannot partake in this rich tradition at home.

It is time to bring storytelling out of the dorms and into the classrooms. Having "Storytelling Week" or "Guest Deaf Storytellers" is not enough. Children need to be doing the telling themselves. They need to learn how to create a personal story and to retell a traditional one. Of course, children cannot be expected to do this without intense exposure to stories read or told to them. But once they are used to what a story is and begin to have an intuitive understanding of how a story works—not by explicit teaching of story elements but rather just by meaningful exposure—the best place to start is "sharing stories about something that happened to them over the weekend; a story about when they were little [or] something that happened to a family member or a friend" (Mallan 1991, 23). Mallan suggests that fables are good jumping-off points because of their clear plots and short length. Cumulative stories, where elements accrue as the stories progress, as well as sequential stories, where one story event is reiterated again and again, also can offer children successful first-time storytelling experiences. She offers a selection of these kinds of stories, as well as ways to assist children in learning the art of storytelling.

By telling stories, children use language for authentic purposes—to keep an audience of their peers interested. To do this, they must create the kind of language that assists their peers in visualizing settings, characters, and actions. This language, gleaned from their exposure to stories watched and read, will be further developed by peers and teachers who genuinely need to have further connection and/or elaboration to fully understand the storyteller's story. Finding out, through conversation, where peers are confused and learning how to use their questions in revamping a particular story, as well as a particular skit or improvisation, will make children more sophisticated language users. This new sophistication eventually will be noted in their understanding of stories written by other authors, as well as in their own creations.

Deaf students also would benefit from the creation of literary works in ASL. Rather than translations or interpretations of works in English, such expression would spring from the artistic or heightened use of ASL grammatical features. Genres could include ASL poetry, ABC stories, and classifier stories. Deaf stories—stories that are unique because they could only happen to a Deaf person (Kuntze 1994, 269)—are also popular components of the literature. However,

> . . . deaf children have not been provided with a language experience comparable to that of their hearing peers, who are routinely exposed to creativity and language-play in school and at home as they grow up. Conditions have yet to be set up in which ASL nursery rhymes and other forms of ASL language-play are cultivated. (270)

It is only recently that works of ASL literature have been eagerly sought by teachers, but the field is new and only a small body of representative work exists. With the respect that ASL has now finally garnered, Deaf poets and writers feel freer to capitalize on the creative components of their language that make it so unique—components that have the potential for creating the same kind of richness and joys for Deaf children that rhyme and chants offer hearing children. In one innovative preschool classroom, "creative ASL time" is reserved for ASL poetry, word plays, and sign games. The teachers of this particular class (one Deaf and the other hearing) report being amazed at how quickly the children pick up on these activities. "Typically, it takes one exposure to an imaginative use of ASL for every child in the group to 'get it.' They love to take turns repeating the poems and plays for their classmates, and eventually take them home to show their parents" (Abrams 1996, 11). I look forward to the time when these creative uses of ASL are more the norm than the exception in the education of Deaf students.

And how and when do we know that what we are doing is working? According to Ann Berthoff (1993), who asks this question of teachers of writing, "We know that what we are doing is working when the response is lively and substantial. We know that this happens only if minds are engaged and that happens only when what our students [do] is seen as dialogic . . . ." (p. 16). If students are participating in engaging talk, if they are part of a lively conversation, then what we are doing is working.

Assessment of Language Users

If students' desires to make and share meaning drive their use of language, it would make sense for any investigation into the assessment of students as language users to describe the success their language has in expressing their intentions. Is a student's language developing to meet her needs for communicating and learning? But what is it specifically that we should be evaluating, in what contexts should we be evaluating it, and who should do the evaluating?

There are certain aspects of language use that enrich a student's language system and interact with her capacity to learn. They are characteristics that people allude to when they refer to articulate, literate speakers and to communication that gets its point across well. They are components of language use that transcend language type and modality, which, therefore, could serve as goals of both oral and written language development for both Deaf and hearing students. They are best described in terms of what students have achieved with language use over a period of time in terms of its quality and, at times, quantity.

One way of viewing these components, adapted from Mayher (1990), might be as follows:

> **Fluency:** How much information is being conveyed? Are longer and more sentences being used to convey more ideas? Do students have the vocabulary for the ideas they wish to convey? Are ideas sustained?
>
> **Complexity:** Are ideas becoming more specific and language more detailed? Are ideas being related to one another?
>
> **Clarity:** Are words used appropriately to mean what they are intended to mean? Is enough information or a particular frame or context provided so that meaning can be shared? Are ideas logically entailed?

Comprehension: How well do students understand the requests and comments of their conversation partners?

An effective way of discerning these signposts of development would be to make brief observational notes of students' use of Sign Language in various classroom contexts. In *The Primary Language Record* (Barrs et al. 1988), a matrix of social and learning contexts is suggested. Social contexts include children in pairs, in a small group, with an adult, in a small/large group with an adult; learning contexts can potentially include any area of the curriculum—during collaborative reading activities (see Chapter 3), at play, or during science investigations. For Deaf students, social contexts would need to be expanded to include both Deaf and hearing teachers, as well as an "other-than-teacher" Deaf adult to catch a glimpse of students in perhaps more comfortable communication situations.

After noting the kind of social and learning contexts, teachers who use *The Primary Language Record* enter brief diary-like notes or anecdotes approximately three times a year about the talking (and listening) their students do. Here is an example:

Dates	Observations and their contexts
1987 Jan	In a group working in the gym (a collaborative group with peers) . . . quickly involved in discussion of the correct way of doing a movement, very forthcoming, explaining her ideas well to others in the group. . . . Quite concerned that a younger child did not grasp my meaning. Took it upon herself to explain in words much simpler and with actions. (37)

These kinds of anecdotal records (although my thinking is that they could be more detailed, with specific reference to the descriptors mentioned previously) reflect current thinking about what good assessment is. If our primary purpose in evaluating language users is to see if language is developing to meet their needs in social and learning contexts, then assessment of it must take place in just those contexts. "The closer the assessment process gets to the student and to the context in which he or she is learning, the more likely it is that this primary purpose will be served" (IRA/NCTE Joint Task Force on Assessment 1994, 16).

Accordingly, it also makes good sense to view teachers as the most important agents of assessment. "Teachers design, assign, observe, collaborate in, and interpret the work of students in their classrooms" (p. 27) six hours a day, five days a week, approximately forty-some-odd weeks a year. There could be no test of language development that could tell anything more validly than the observations of teachers with those credentials.

Of course, I am well aware that some attention also needs to be given to the structural side of language use. Teachers, and particularly parents, of young Deaf children need to be aware of the kinds of grammatical knowledge their students/children have or are coming to know and to see the development over time of grammatical processes and structures. A possible framework for thinking about structural development is in Livingston, 1983. At the writing of this book, Judith Mounty, of the Educational Testing Service in Princeton, New Jersey, is designing a checklist of Sign Language Development to assess and monitor the acquisition of ASL grammar by children.

To assess the development of structural growth, it would be helpful for school staff members who are thoroughly well-versed in the linguistic structure of ASL to gather samples of students using ASL in various social and learning contexts toward the beginning and end of each school term. These staff members might unobtrusively observe classes to record the kinds of ASL grammatical processes and features (as well as the kinds of features representative of contact signing) individual students display, noting the contexts within which they are created. If this data is compiled for several grades, teachers and parents would have a much better perspective on what Deaf children are capable of doing structurally with language and when they are capable of doing it.

I have always been amazed at how little has been done in schools for Deaf students to adequately and appropriately assess Sign Language development. I think the reason for the inaction is the desire of teachers and administrators to have *the definitive test of language competence*—standardized and field-tested—and because there has been none developed, everyone is sitting back waiting for it to appear. As with most authentic assessments, however, the most valuable "tests" can be found right in teachers' own backyards—in their own classrooms where language can be assessed in familiar contexts and over time. How nice it would finally be to speak realistically and with confidence about the path of Sign Language development in Deaf students.

Chapter Three

Becoming Better Readers

Different Linguistic Experiences . . . Less Than Optimum Teaching Methodologies

Kindergarten and first-grade teachers are well aware of how hearing children learn to read effortlessly and well. In the years before school, they have garnered a plethora of world knowledge and an impressive command of language. They have had myriad opportunities to hear stories told and read that enable them to enhance their knowledge and develop an understanding of the way stories work and an "ear" for the language used to tell them. Upon arrival at school, practice with the nitty-gritty mechanics of learning to read—word identification, page and line navigation, and opportunities to read books of their own choosing—more or less completes what is needed for hearing children to be called beginning readers.

Lay people unfamiliar with the education of Deaf children are often perplexed about why Deaf children, particularly of hearing parents, encounter difficulties learning to read (after all, they are not visually impaired). But there are differences—some obvious, others not so obvious—between the quality of linguistic experiences such children and hearing children bring to the task of learning to read. Consider a Memorial Day parade I took my daughter to when she was three and a half years old. There was much that she experienced visually—marching soldiers, balloons blowing in the wind, people waving and clapping, policemen requesting onlookers to stay behind barricades. There was also much that she questioned that was responded to with language at a level within her frame of reference: Those soldiers fought against mean people to help make good people safe; those are Girl Scouts, they go on hikes, learn how to sew, and sell cookies to earn money for the cloth and thread they need. In addition to the relevant vocabulary my daughter was being exposed to, she was being exposed to explanation—the "what fors" and "whys" behind the visual experience—which serves to both enlighten and extend visual experience. This was just one episode among thousands where she had the opportunity to begin to become knowledgeable and "stockpile" that knowledge for subsequent encounters with words such as *soldiers* and *Girl Scouts* in later life, including reading.

Deaf children growing up in homes where Sign is not used predominantly and fluently possess a wealth of visual experience that remains linguistically unrepresented. Such experience remains private and, as such, unable to be shared, explained, or expanded upon by a wider audience. When visual experience lies fallow and thereby untouched for further growth and development, there is little opportunity to become knowledgeable at an early age. Subsequent encounters with words during later reading will call for simultaneous knowledge creation, making the teaching of reading a decidedly slower process for Deaf children of nonsigning parents than for hearing children.

Young hearing and Deaf children also have vastly different opportunities to "hear" stories read "aloud." What is a common occurrence in most hearing middle-class households is uncommon in households where parents are hearing and children are Deaf, primarily because of the language barriers between parent and child. Although there are many hearing parents who sign to their Deaf children, most often their competence in Sign is insufficient to meet the demands of text-based language where sentence structure can be complicated, vocabulary specialized, and figurative language abundant. Most middle-class hearing children have had hundreds if not thousands of books read to them prior to entry into school; the number is nowhere near that for Deaf children of hearing parents.

The repercussions are at least twofold. With exposure to hundreds if not thousands of books, hearing children are exposed to hundreds if not thousands of words and, concomitantly, hundreds if not thousands of new ideas. Such children do not need extended explanation of most words they encounter later in print. If they cannot either decode a word or figure out its meaning from context, they are told it, most often know the meaning of it because it is part of their listening/speaking vocabularies, and proceed with their reading. For Deaf children without large watching/signing vocabularies, telling will not necessarily mean knowing, and independent reading may quickly turn into extended vocabulary discussions where, at times, concepts will need to be created from scratch.

Children who are read to are also simultaneously exposed to the ways stories work—that beginnings are entailed in endings, that problems happen to characters, that resolutions occur. Experienced story listeners/watchers can predict endings or what might happen, next which propels them through stories. They can hang on until problems are resolved and the point of a story is made. Inexperienced story listeners/watchers tend to view each picture as a separate entity without any relation to an overall point. They see few relationships from picture to picture because their concept of story is only in the process of being formed. Such children will have difficulty writing and even telling stories.

Read-to children also start to become comfortable with the "sound" of text—how longer and more complex ideas tend to have distinct intonational patterns. They get used to having to listen longer so that words at beginnings and endings of sentences can gel into a particular meaning. It is not uncommon for hearing children to hear the same stories over and over—further fortifying sound-text connections.

Although there are differences in the language that hearing children bring to learning to read and the language that appears in books (i.e., the use of dialogue and narration, literary phrases, and more complex syntax), for the most part, the language they have mastered is a fairly close approximation to the language they need to know to become beginning readers. In addition, although there have been continuing debates as to the role that phonics plays in learning to read, there can be little doubt that a sound-based language is more conducive to learning how to read than one that is not. Although "sounding out" is not the primary way most young hearing children learn how to recognize words (nor should it be), to some extent, children do call upon their graphophonemic knowledge when tackling new words. This knowledge, along with hints from the context of what is being read, in addition to some remembrance of words or word-parts from contexts past, propels hearing children on with their reading. And if the ideas conveyed in books being read are both well-pictured and within their frames of reference, this "decoding" will result in meaningful reading.

When Deaf children begin learning how to read, the language they bring to text in no way resembles the language of which they are called upon to make meaning. For the most part, their language employs the grammatical processes of ASL, but is severely restricted in the breadth of its syntax and lexicon. If any English-like signing exists, it, too, is rudimentary. And because Sign is a visual-gestural language, "sounding out" and decoding print are meaningless activities. Young Deaf children unfamiliar with using context to help figure out the meaning of words cannot easily make meaning of words that are new to them. Either they fingerspell them—which does not mean that they understand them unless the words are within their fingerspelling lexicons (where they are unlikely to be since most schools downplay its use)—or ask what they are. Only as Deaf children become older and more able readers does context begin to play a part in helping them make meaning from words that are new to them.

There should be little disagreement, then, that Deaf and hearing children bring different linguistic experiences to learning to read, differences that need to be addressed as quickly and as effectively as possible. Responsibility for this most often falls squarely on the shoulders of schools for Deaf children. Although there is no doubt that these schools have produced some good readers, less-than-effective teaching methodologies have prevented them from producing more and better readers. It is not uncommon for many educators of Deaf children to consider the language-learning that transpires prior to formal schooling as a strict prerequisite, and to delay the teaching of reading until the children "have language"—most often meaning some degree of proficiency with spoken, signed, or written English. Their thinking here is that Deaf children need to produce English before they can read English. The formal teaching of reading, then, is "back-burnered" and replaced with a combination of direct language teaching (i.e., sentence construction) and language experience work under the guise of reading instruction sometimes well into the middle-elementary grades. Although there is nothing wrong with language experience work, children do not become readers by indulging in a steady diet of it by itself. The many tales of Deaf students who say they were never given books to read throughout high school are not exceptional examples.

Nor do Deaf students become readers indulging in a steady diet of reading series prepared specifically for them. Such books have little, if any, story to convey. Written by educators of Deaf children as opposed to real authors, their primary intention is to build vocabulary and familiarity with specific sentence parts and patterns rather than to engage children in finding out "what happens" in a story appropriate to their common emotional experiences. Much like the "back-burnering" of the teaching of reading discussed previously, the rationale behind the creation of such books stems from the mistaken notion that Deaf children must first learn sentence structure before reading real books. There has and still continues to be little faith in the notion that early meaningful reading opportunities will fortify and strengthen linguistic competencies in general (Williams 1994).

Few hearing teachers know how to read a story to Deaf children in a way that is meaningful to them. Most often text is signed following strict English word order. Sign choices are sign-for-word glosses as opposed to ASL interpretations of text, leaving children who are only at the beginning stages of learning the workings of English at a loss as to the point of a story. Many schools for Deaf children have a paucity of good story-reading role models who are skilled at capturing young audiences through the expert use of ASL.

And it is just this unfamiliarity with the workings of ASL that adversely affects not only the way stories are read to Deaf children but also the way reading is actually taught. It is the rare hearing teacher who can "track" print in guided reading situations while keeping the integrity of Sign. Most reading lessons turn into word-for-sign translations of text, which substitute one form of English (written) for another (signed). Unless meaningful Sign is used to *interpret* text, Deaf students will continue to be stymied by written English. Limbrick et al. (1992) also sees fundamental problems with the teaching of reading in schools for Deaf students—insufficient time is devoted to it compared to the time devoted to it in schools for hearing students; instruction is not grounded in thorough knowledge of the process of reading.

Although there certainly are differences in the linguistic experiences that Deaf children bring to learning to read, they are exacerbated by less-than-effective teaching practices that account for the fact that more Deaf students are not better readers. Such history, however, is not set in stone. With more appropriate methodologies, more Deaf students will become better readers and they will avoid the frustration experienced by Abel in Greenberg's (1970) *In This Sign*. Raised without Sign in the early twentieth century, the omniscient narrator describes what reading is like for Abel as a grown man:

> The newspaper had been an affectation at first and a defense against having to stare at people on the bus, but since he had come to be a leader in the Deaf community and someone to be consulted, he had come to know the few well-educated Deaf, in the city, people who spelled more than they Signed because their needs and knowledges exceeded the Signs that were used for the basic things of living. More and more he felt himself needing to grow into these new words. How complicated they were! How minutely subtle the differences they could express! As he watched these Deaf he began to understand dimly some of the joy they felt in their arrival at the perfect meaning, the exact word, the shade of difference between "discipline" and "punishment," between "respectful" and "respectable." He had begun to try to read the newspaper and later had even bought a dictionary by which he

hoped to be made able to understand it. . . .Nevertheless, although he did not admit it to Janice, the dictionary had been a mistake. It embarrassed him even while he blundered and stumbled over the words that were supposed to explain the other words—when he was through, the words had sieved all meaning and left him with nothing. . . .This evening he was glad to be free of his house and vanish into the hunt. He settled back in his chair with that dictionary and the *National News*. Mr. Truman had made a statement about his position on an arms treaty. Abel sighed. *Position*. He had struggled with *arms* in the newspaper before. There were times, Mr. Walker from Church had told him, that *arms* did not really-mean arms, but guns and cannons, bombs—things that neither looked, worked, nor acted like arms, and were not part of a man's body. Nevertheless. *Treaty*. The word was under *treat* and right under *treatment*. "The act of treating or negotiating for the adjustment of differences." None of the words but *treating* and *difference* meant anything, and the s on the end of difference made him suspicious of it. The President was talking like a doctor about treating, so the arms must be body arms after all. (204-205)

Abel was attempting to be like what he himself calls the "Two-World Deaf"—"the rare, beautifully Signing, well-educated Deaf who did not consider reading an activity for hearing alone . . .and began to wonder if he might be able to reach their worldliness" (p. 204). For Abel, who grew up at perhaps the wrong time and perhaps in the wrong place, the worldliness quest might be beyond his reach. But for Deaf children today, there is little need to wonder about worldliness if afforded appropriate learning experiences. Delayed language development notwithstanding, Deaf children can become strong readers when ASL is put to use in literacy contexts that are meaning-driven.

Reading Aloud

I remember attending an international conference on research within the field of ASL not too long ago and being pleasantly surprised by the last speaker's presentation. Rather than a "paper," Harlan Lane read an excerpt from his book, *The Wild Boy of Aveyron* (1979). As he read, the audience did not stir, and when he finished, I don't think anyone realized that more than thirty minutes had elapsed. We were all in a trance. Not only was this a breath of fresh air from the lectures of the prior days, it had a much greater impact on us. We were moved to another place and time when we entered the lives of Victor and Itard. We felt for and connected with these characters. We saw them in our minds; we grew to know them. At the conclusion of the read-aloud, conference participants breathed deeply and stretched. We had been through an emotional experience and were starting to re-enter present time and the conference room.

We should read aloud to Deaf children to offer precisely these kinds of feelings—to take them from the here-and-now and transport them to a different place and time where they can meet new characters and experience the "what happens" in their lives—for the sheer pleasure it affords. We want them to breathe deeply and stretch after they have watched a story as proof that they have been somewhere else for a while. We want them to be entertained and mesmerized by what they have seen.

There are, of course, important byproducts of these trance-like states. The most obvious is the new insight or knowledge that they provide. When children make an emotional connection with a story, they take something away from it—something that hooks them and makes it difficult to forget. The more they are hooked, the more they are learning and the more this learning carries over into different arenas of their lives. "This is like in the story _____." "I did it just like the girl in _____." "I got my idea from the story about _____." As Jim Trelease (1989) says, reading aloud—and he speaks primarily about fiction—is the best way to teach children about most anything because its context is a slice of life—there is almost always something for children to relate to in a good book. Other important byproducts seem to confirm what educational researchers have discovered over the past twenty years—children who have been read to are better independent readers. This makes sense for reasons already discussed on pages 46–47: Children who are experienced story listeners/watchers have larger vocabularies and a better developed sense of story structure. They are used to "book-words and phrases" and the ways authors create characters and conflict.

But if we stick to our primary purpose for reading aloud to Deaf children—to provide an emotional experience that hooks them into finding out what happens—they will soon be tempted to find out what happens for themselves: the beginning step in making them lifelong independent readers, perhaps *the* most important byproduct of reading aloud to them. However, none of these byproducts will actualize if Deaf children are not read aloud to properly. There is little joy in watching a story that fails to make them breathe deeply and stretch at its completion because of the way it is told.

Reading Aloud to Deaf Children at Different Ages

What and how you read aloud to all children—Deaf or hearing—will vary according to their age. For toddlers and children through the age of three or four with attention spans in the process of becoming longer, selections should not be too lengthy. At these ages, and for some considerable time thereafter, depending on the linguistic maturity of the children, Deaf children will derive most of a selection's meaning from its pictures. Reading aloud becomes a kind of conversation between adult and child about what is happening in the pictures; the story line or message in the text (again, depending on the audience and how clearly the story's point is pictured) may or may not be conveyed. The pictures are more "talked about" than read about. As an example, here is an excerpt from a dialogue between a hearing mother and her hearing twenty-three-month-old as they "read aloud" from Eric Hill's Spot's First Walk (1981).

Text: *What have you found?*

Child: What's the dog doing?

Mom: He's digging in the dirt looking for his bone. Look what he found there.

Child: Oh.

Mom (reading the text): *What have you found, Spot?*

Child: A doggy bone.

Mom: Yes, he's found a doggy bone. He's having fun outside.

Child: Yeah.

Mom: What is he doing with his feet?

Child: What's he doing with his feet, Mom?

Mom: He's digging.

Child: He's digging. (Altwerger, Diehl-Faxon, and Dockstade-Anderson as cited in Trelease 1989, 45)

It is the picture that captivates the child and conversation about it involves him, thereby sustaining his interest.

In her study of the reading behavior of Alice, a two-year-old Deaf child of Deaf parents, Madeline Maxwell (1984) made special note of the way Alice's father read aloud to her. She states,

> . . . at the picture of the old woman making the gingerbread boy, for example, Father pointed to the picture and signed COOK, ROLL-OUT-DOUGH, making the latter sign over the pictured dough. When the illustration showed the gingerbread boy running by and waving at a bear, Father pointed to the pictured bear and signed BEAR PRO BEAR PRO BITE, using the pictured boy instead of his other hand as the object of bite. . . . Father thus transfers the spatial relations of ASL manual signs to the objects in the pictures so that a picture substitutes for a usual sign location. (199)

For Deaf children just at the beginning stages of language acquisition, signing on, to, and from pictures in storybooks makes sense. It capitalizes on what they know (the pictures they are looking at) and offers them new understanding (the meaning inherent in the picture in symbolic form, sign language) in understandable small doses. The point is that the pictures should lead or direct the hands. Predictable books where happenings are repeated with slight variation throughout the book and simple wordless picture books work well with this age group. Suggestions for such books are in Kimmel and Segal (1991) and Trelease (1989, 1992).

As children become older and more linguistically competent, perhaps at the kindergarten through second- or third-grade level, story lines can be conveyed in the air. What is advocated is *text interpretation,* wherein the text on each page is processed and reformulated according to the reader's estimation of what it takes for her children to understand the author's intent. Once this meaning has been created, it needs to be conveyed via the picture on the page, by either pointing out who or what is being referred to or stepping into a particular character's role by shifting to a similar position as the pictured character. In addition, use of several *interpretation strategies* may be helpful in assisting students in understanding the story line (these strategies are described on pages 56–59). The crucially important point, however, is that teachers must know the story prior to interpreting it. They must know the meaning as expressed in the storyline on each page so that appropriate interpretations into Sign can be created to convey the meaning of the text more visually. Reading and signing at the same time should be avoided because what results is English in Sign, which for young Deaf children is still very much a foreign language.

Criteria for book selection at this level might be as follows: Content should appeal to the particular age group being read to and should consider their common emotional experiences; ideas conveyed should be within children's frames of reference and pictures should represent most, if not all, of the meaning of the text. If these criteria are fulfilled, there will be little need to worry about the sentence length or syntactic complexity of the language of the text; interest in the topic, familiarity with it, pictures and, most important, a good interpretation, will carry children through the story. Remember also that there is nothing wrong with shortening long, descriptive passages for children whose attention spans are still in the process of developing and that fiction need not be the only genre for read-alouds—there is a plethora of well-pictured, nonfiction books that capture the imaginations of young children, as described in Kobrin (1988).

As children become older, they become more linguistically competent and are able to understand increasingly complex stories. Most often these stories are accompanied by more lines of text per pictured page. The task of the reader/interpreter, then, becomes more demanding—even more demanding than that faced by voice-to-

Sign interpreters because reader/interpreters also need to decode (i.e., identify words in) a written text. They also need to juggle eye movements between text and audience if they expect to engage their audience at all.

To have a model of what reading aloud looks like at this stage, I asked John, a fourth-generation Deaf parent, to read Dayal Kaur Khalsa's (1987) *I Want a Dog* "aloud" to his two Deaf children, Mike, seven, and Annie, nine. As with most of the stories he reads aloud to his children, this was a first-time read-aloud—it was not practiced—much the way stories are read to children by most parents. *I Want a Dog*, a beautifully pictured book with from one to twelve sentences per page, describes the attempt of May, a young girl, to convince her parents to buy her a dog. She demonstrates how responsible she would be by taking good care of a pretend dog: a rollerskate tied to a string.

John sat on Annie's bed with his back leaning against the wall. Both Annie and Mike sat on John's left side, angled slightly toward John. John held the opened picture-book in his left hand slightly angled toward the children while he signed the text with his right hand only. However, at times he used his left wrist and upper arm as the base hand for signs that most often require two articulators, such as TAKE-CARE-OF, WITH, WORLD, MORE, and MEAN. There were also times when he just signed these two-handed signs with one hand in the air without any support from the arm holding the book. When he would expound upon a point in the story or when he would perform mimetic signs (DOGS-JUMP-ALL-OVER), he would rest the book on his knees and sign with both hands.

John mouthed most individual signs and used specific mouth movements found in ASL for words such as COOL, PATIENT, and EASY. Mouth movements were eliminated for mimetic signs such as JUMP-ALL-OVER, SAVE-MONEY-IN-BANK, MONEY-INCREASE, and DOG-RUN-AROUND-TEAR-UP-THINGS and added to finger-spelled words to complete a phrase, as when the words *do it* were mouthed after the sign CAN was performed. For the word *vet*, John mouthed *vet* but signed DOCTOR. For the words *on the day*, John signed DAY as he simultaneously mouthed *one day*.

Adhering to the order of the text—essentially a transliteration of it—happened more at the beginning of the reading than in the middle or toward the end because John was being videotaped and was a little bit nervous and self-conscious. This transliteration happened most often, but not exclusively, while John was reading the text and signing what he was reading at the exact same time. This makes sense because John was not allowing himself any processing time to create equivalencies in ASL. When he did allow himself time, by reading ahead one or two sentences, his signing became more ASL-like and more interpretive, as seen in the following:

(1)

Text: But every time she asked her parents if she could have a dog, they said, "No."

eye gaze upwards

Signed: EVERY TIME SHE ASK+++ PARENTS, HEY, ME CAN HAVE DOG/ PARENTS SAY-NO++

(2)

Text: She remembered when she had first tried to rollerskate. She kept falling down, but her father told her, "If at first you don't succeed, try, try, try again." And that's what she had always done. Now she *could* rollerskate. May decided to try another way to get a dog.

Signed: TRY+++ ROLLERSKATE EVENTUAL-SUCCESS

eyes_____forward

SAME-THERE-HERE/ DOG TRY "ask" MOTHER FATHER "ask++ "/ MAYBE CAN GET DOG LATER

(3)

Text: That evening her parents decided it was time to settle the dog question once and for all.

Signed: NOW THAT NIGHT MOTHER FATHER DECIDE TIME SIT-AS-GROUP

rhet-q

WITH MAY ABOUT DOG/ WHAT

(4)

Text: She ran to the store, tossed her rollerskate's leash around a tree, and rushed in.

Signed: FIRST DOG ROPE-AROUND-TREE TIE-TIGHT/LEAVE FINISH, ROLLERSKATE LEAVE rt /RUN-IN

In Example 1, John read ahead rather imperceptibly and decided to step into the character of May. He changed an indirect request into a direct one by becoming May, through the use of eye gaze direction and having May formulate the question herself. In Example 2, the subtext is that May is planning to be as persistent in getting her dog as she was in learning how to rollerskate. John interpreted the text fairly straightforwardly, then paused to reread it. This rereading allowed him to better process its intent and formulate a more explicit interpretation, as shown in the example. In Example 3, his signing mimicked the way May and her parents were sitting in the living room. Adding the rhetorical question *WHAT* let his children in on the fact that some explaining was in the offering. In Example 4, John decided that meaning would be better portrayed via mimetic blends, a more clearly delineated time sequence, and repeated use of the verb LEAVE.

These interpretations of text required processing time on John's part and there were pauses in his reading as he first approached them. He read ahead in the text and decided that the ideas inherent in it could best be conveyed via certain features of ASL, as well as certain interpretation strategies (see pages 56–59), based on his estimation of what would make sense to his children. Sometimes he read and transliterated at the same time, then stopped himself, realizing that what he signed could be signed more meaningfully, and re-signed the text as in Example 2. These read-ahead times or when he searched for better equivalent meanings transpired smoothly and without a hint of fidgeting or impatience on the part of his children.

Interpretation Strategies

Of particular interest was the number of times John left the text to add to it. These additions, which I am calling *interpretation strategies*, were for very specific reasons. The most frequently occurring addition served to overtly state the implied points in the text. There were twenty-four instances of this kind of addition, which were categorized under the heading *Explicitness*. In the following examples, all additions listed are interpretations of John's ASL as performed by a certified interpreter.

Text: She tied a rope around the rollerskate and pulled. . . .She walked across the room with it. The rollerskate rolled after her. It was just like walking a dog on a leash.

Addition (Explicitness): Understand? She pulled the rollerskate around as if it were a real dog and in her imagination it felt like a real puppy.

Text: After that, May and her rollerskate were never apart.

Addition (Explicitness): . . .because she was afraid of losing it like she lost it before. She kept it close.

John was ensuring that his children were understanding the subtext of the message; in these examples, the reasons behind May's actions. Such explanation served to tighten connections among the different parts of the story.

John also reiterated certain points rather prevalently—seventeen times. In the following examples, it appears that the reason for this was to emphasize an idea. This strategy is called *Reiteration*.

Text: May, though, wanted a dog *right now*.

Addition (Reiteration): Not later.

Text: And every day, in rain or sleet or hail or snow, May took her rollerskate for a walk.

Addition (Reiteration): Boy, she takes the rollerskate out with her even in bad weather.

There were times (ten) when John departed from the text to supply a real-world connection for his children. In the following example, the idea inherent in the text was explained by providing the background knowledge necessary to understand it. This strategy is called *Providing Background Knowledge*.

Text: When she got home that afternoon she ran right to the refrigerator and grabbed a thick slice of salami. She went outside and began strolling slowly down the street. Every dog on the block jumped up as May walked by.

Addition (Providing Background Knowledge): Salami. . .you know, meat. You know because dogs love salami.

Text: For this one she needed to save up all her allowance.

Addition (Providing Background Knowledge): You know parents give their kids a dollar or two each week and they can save it.

John also "brought the story home" for his children by relating events to their own lives, as seen in the following example *Relating Text to Children's Experiences*. He used this strategy six times.

Text: "They have to be walked every morning and every night," her father said.

Addition (Relating Text to Children's Experiences): Can you two hold it all day? Can you imagine taking the dog out and bringing it back before you go to school in the morning?

There is perhaps no better way for children to connect with a story than to see how a character's plight would play out in their own lives. The thought of walking the dog in the early morning hours before school vividly conveys one of the inconveniences May's parents were trying to establish.

John made reference to the pictures in the storybook most often before interpreting the text on the same page. The reference usually either called the children's attention to certain aspects of the picture or was a comment about it. This use of pictures differs dramatically from the way pictures need to be used with younger Deaf children, as discussed previously. Here, signing on or to and from pictures was only rarely done because story meaning was being conveyed primarily via Sign only. Examples of *Picture Reference* follow; they occurred ten times.

Picture Context: "Rollerskate dog" is tied to a tree outside a restaurant.

Picture Reference: Now do you see where she left the dog?

Picture Context: May's classmates in school all with dog faces instead of human faces.

Picture Reference: Maybe she's imagining this.

These interpretation strategies transpired rather effortlessly. We can assume that John felt the need to make these additions to both engage and convey meaning to his children; it was obvious that he was successful at both. His children hardly stirred during the read-aloud and, at its conclusion, were able to penetrate to the heart of the story as evidenced by a simple retelling and reaction.

Interpreting text into one language from another simultaneously as one reads it is a complicated task requiring a plethora of processing behaviors. It should come as no surprise, then, that during the read-aloud, portions of the text were deleted. There were times when I was not quite sure if John had processed the meaning thoroughly enough for himself and, perhaps realizing this, opted to delete the text. In one instance, John misinterpreted a portion of the text; when he was faced with the following segment that needed the misinterpreted portion for it to make sense, he deleted the second segment. There were other instances where deletions were purposeful. Several months after the tape was made, I asked John why he deleted specific parts of the text. He said that he sometimes eliminates "details" that he judges not to be integral to the story line in an effort to limit distracting "verbiage." He also said that he sometimes deletes sentences that are clearly pictured. Examples of *Deletions* that can be considered "detail" deletions are exemplified as follows:

Text: May decided to try another way to get a dog. For this one she needed to save up all her allowance. *When the day she had been planning for finally arrived*, she went out and bought everything she needed. . .

Text: She built a giant training course where she could practice walking her rollerskate. "We're so happy to see you busy *doing something other than always trying to get a dog*," her parents told her.

It is important to note that deletions occur in the work of the best voice-to-Sign interpreters (Livingston, Singer, and Abramson 1994)—a much less demanding task than being a reader/interpreter—and that when hearing parents read stories to young children, they too delete information that tends to be overly descriptive or abstract. Incredibly interesting are the similarities that exist between John as a reader/interpreter and the ASL interpreters in the Livingston et al. study of interpretation effectiveness described in Chapters 1 (pp. 4–6) and 2 (pp. 33–36). John inherently knew that being explicit, repeating ideas for emphasis, providing background knowledge, and even deleting some text were ways to better connect his children with the story. These exact kinds of strategies—in addition to several others—were employed by professional ASL interpreters whose interpretations afforded their audiences greater understanding of two oral presentations given by college teachers.

There is much to be learned, then, from analyzing the work of Deaf people functioning as text interpreters, as well as the work of effective voice-to-Sign hearing ASL interpreters, when looking for models of reading aloud to Deaf students. It is heartening to note that researchers have turned their attention to descriptive studies of the specific strategies that Deaf mothers (Andrews and Taylor 1987; Lartz and Lestina 1995) and native signing teachers (Mather 1990) use as they read aloud to Deaf children. These are research results that are helpful to hearing teachers and parents.

Reading aloud should not end when children are beyond the picture-book stage. Today picture books are used in middle-school, high-school, and college classrooms, particularly in writing classrooms that are theme-based or where the style of a particular author is being scrutinized. However, although pictures help to cast a spell, they are not a prerequisite when reading aloud to older audiences. As children progress through the upper-elementary grades and into junior and senior high school, good-quality chapter books, short stories, and excerpts from novels can be read aloud.

But the task becomes even more complicated when text does not come in a few lines and short paragraphs and when there are no pictures for linguistic backup for the students. If you are a competent signer, there is no reason to not read aloud using the strategies discussed herein with the realization that as text becomes more complicated and distanced from the audience, more read-ahead time will be needed so that text can be interpreted meaningfully. While Deaf teachers will not have any difficulty with this, especially if the reading is familiar, I suggest that less sign-experienced hearing teachers team up with sign-experienced hearing teachers so the latter can be solely the interpreter as the former reads the story out loud, more closely approximating the speaker/interpreter situation.

Criteria for book selection for older students are the same as those for younger students, barring the necessity of having books that are well-pictured: selections should be engaging, embodying content that appeals to their common emotional experiences. Linda Reif's (1992) list of books best-liked by her junior high school students might be a good place to start a search for engaging books. Mysteries are always a favorite and work well when they are read aloud a little each day.

If students are afforded just fifteen minutes a day of quality read-aloud time, in a short time you will notice differences in their vocabulary and conceptual growth. You will notice them making references to what they have read and noting similarities and differences between ideas they encounter in their lives and those in the books read to them. Younger children's play and their art creations will be influenced by these new learnings as well. These are all indications that true learning has transpired; again, this learning will not happen if books are read aloud improperly. What we have learned from John is that quality read-alouds encompass interpretation judgments based on knowing the audience being read to, as well as the linguistic and informational demands of what is being read. With this knowledge in the hands of an expert signer, we can begin to provide Deaf children the kinds of read-aloud experiences they deserve.

Teaching Reading

Marie Clay's (1972) statistics on hearing first-grade readers are rather sobering to teachers of Deaf students. According to Clay, superior hearing readers in the first grade average reading twenty thousand words during their first year of reading instruction, average readers ten to fifteen thousand, and slow readers five thousand. How many words do Deaf readers read during their first year of instruction? Although I have never come across any published number, from my experience I would venture to say that the number does not exceed five hundred. And that is being very generous.

While acknowledging the role that letter-sound knowledge plays in assisting hearing children in learning these thousands of words, many reading theorists today tend to downplay its significance; instead, they talk about mental representations of words or the stockpile of words that readers keep in their heads and recognize on sight and use to compare with new words encountered (Goswami 1986; Tunmer and Nesdale 1985). Interestingly, hearing children who are adept at sounding out pseudowords are not children who receive formal instruction in letter-sound correspondence, but rather those who know more real print words with which to compare the pseudowords. It appears to be strictly the numbers of words in a child's mental lexicon that broadens the choices from which analogies to other words and word-parts can be made (Moustafa 1993). Learning letter-sound correspondences, then, while helpful for hearing children learning to read, is neither prerequisite nor crucial for them to become readers.

Such is the case of learning to read a nonalphabetic language such as Chinese. Rather than learning how to put sounds together to say words, Chinese characters are already words or parts of words. They do not need to be decoded into separable parts, only learned as a whole. And such is the case for the majority of profoundly Deaf people who are competent readers. When learning to read, they surely did not decode, because letter-sound correspondences are meaningless to most profoundly Deaf people, but rather learned word-sign equivalents. The implication is clear: The major hurdle in learning to read—in any language—is creating a rich mental lexicon of words in print. Despite the differences, then, in the languages that hearing and Deaf children bring to the task of learning to read, they should learn to read in much the same way—by being provided with meaningful exposure to reading—and lots of it.

This simple fact has gone unnoticed until very recently. What has been noticed are the ways Deaf readers "recode" (i.e., change words into mouth movements, fingerspelling, or signs) and recall text (Treiman and Hirsh-Pasek 1983), how they integrate text information (Marschark, De Beni, Polazzo, and Cornoldi 1993), and how well they remember text verbatim (Kelly 1993). From this work we have learned, respectively, that skilled Deaf readers recode printed words either via mouth movements or Sign; that Deaf readers are less likely than hearing readers to see how idea units are related in extended text; and that skilled Deaf readers remember more words that comprise test sentences than less-skilled Deaf readers.

Although these findings may fascinate psychologists who seek to distinguish differences in text-processing between auditory/oral and visual/gestural modalities, they are of little help to teachers who seek better ways of teaching Deaf children to read. With years of research in this area (Kelly 1990), it is time for researchers to consider the possibility that differences in reading abilities might be due more to differences in exposure to meaningful reading instruction than processing differences. The key to assisting Deaf students in becoming better readers might better be looked for in the homes of students who are good readers, as well as in the classrooms of teachers who know how Deaf students learn to read and how to teach reading well.

Text Interpretation

Deaf children learn to read by having text interpreted for them. The two key words are *text* and *interpreted;* with respect to text, for far too long there has not been enough of it. This travesty is in large part responsible for the inexperience of so many young Deaf readers—they simply are not given enough to read. As corroborated by Limbrick, McNaughton, and Clay (1992), Deaf children do not engage in reading in school as much as hearing children do. For years, teacher-preparation programs have advocated excluding the use of print in nursery and kindergarten classes, fearing that it would distract young children from lipreading and learning speech. As such, it was the rare nursery teacher who labelled students' drawings—a simple beginning reading activity that has been going on for decades in schools for hearing children.

There is additionally the problem of text appropriateness. Deaf children, also for too long, have not been reading the kinds of books that hearing children have. Although there is a case for the exclusion of books that rhyme, there seems to be little rationale for excluding the plethora of "beginning reader" books available for young hearing children. The majority of these books are designed with the needs of the beginning reader in mind:

Subject matter embodies the common experiences of young children; ideas conveyed are clearly reflected in pictures; stories are short; most often there is repetition and thereby predictability about events to come; and sentence length increases with competence of the reader (see Appendix A for suggested titles). These books do not have hidden agendas. They are, first and foremost, engaging stories and, second, simply conveyed. They are not, first and foremost, ways of exposing children to vocabulary or sentence patterns and, second, a contrived story embodying those characteristics. These kinds of books, especially those created specifically for Deaf children, too often are found on classroom shelves.

Young children should start with books that they can handle in a sitting—approximately five to ten minutes. Big print size is helpful and, for the beginner, two, three, or four words per sentence fit the bill. Books chosen can be those with which the children are familiar (i.e., books read to them; books they choose to look at on their own) or those that they are seeing for the first time. If the book is new to them, they will need time to "know the pictures"—before calling their attention to the text, give them plenty of time to take in the happenings in the pictures. Most often children will have something to say about each picture. They should have the opportunity to do so. However, when it is time for them to follow the text for the first time, it is the teacher's—and no one else's— turn.

The second key word mentioned was *interpreted*; here we need to think carefully about our purpose—to teach Deaf children how to read, to assist them in creating print-Sign equivalences that make sense to them. For young children just beginning to read, because text is simple and its meaning is clearly conveyed in pictures, there is no reason why they wouldn't be able to follow simple interpretations of text where the order of the text is followed but sign choices are made from the ASL lexicon. This kind of interpretation differs in purpose from that discussed in the reading-aloud section. In reading aloud, our purpose is to share an author's intent via pictures and ASL. In teaching reading, our purpose is to share an author's intent via pictures, printed words, and the kind of Sign that assists students in making meaning out of words as they read them. However, just as John—our Deaf model who read more complicated text aloud and "cold"—seemed to intuitively know when to use ASL and when to stay close to the text, so should teachers of reading when they are guiding students. This is another instance of where teachers need to become artistic interpreters (as described in Chapter 2).

For teachers trained to sign exact renditions of English words and morphemes while communicating, the goal of staying close to the text while preserving the integrity of the ASL lexicon can be problematic. Should words and signs always correspond one-to-one? What role does word meaning play in choosing corresponding signs? (Obviously not as sizeable a consideration in printed-spoken word correspondence, where so many words are pronounced in only one way yet have myriad meanings; e.g., fly, drive, run, play.) In short, how exactly is this print-to-Sign interpretation accomplished?

Let's begin with some examples from the nursery school. The best way to ensure that word-sign interpretations will be meaningful is to focus on meaning that children have already created for themselves. Children love to tell teachers what their drawings or paintings are about (what they already know); these descriptions/explanations should be converted into print in front of the child. Even before the issue of interpretation is addressed, however, there are questions that take priority. How much of what the child says should teachers write? How "book-like" should the language be? Because the goal is to have the child read back the label after it is read by the teacher, for the very beginning reader, labels should be short and simple and written as an almost exact repetition of what the child signed in order for them to be more easily read back and understood. They should, however, be in English.

As examples, if a very beginning reader signs, MOTHER MY about her picture, the label might be *My mother*. The child would sign MY and then MOTHER as the teacher points, in this case, to one word at a time. This should be reread by the child. Rereading is crucially important as it will help children remember what the words mean. For children who are beginning to show an interest in words and books, it might be helpful to move them along toward more text-like language. For example, if this is signed:

PT [to picture] ME SCHOOL V-CL'walk to school'

about a picture showing a child walking to school, an appropriate label might be, *This is me walking to school*. The word *This* can be pointed to with one finger while the other finger is pointing to the picture. ME might be signed by the child pointing his own index finger to himself. *Walking to* might be signed as exemplified previously as the teacher sweeps across the words with her index finger (signing *to* is not necessary because its meaning is incorporated in the execution of the sign as transcribed) and the sign for *school* follows. More than likely, when the child rereads the label on his own, he will either spell or sign *is* and *to* or request signs for them. Requests such as these should be honored.

The important points are to keep the captions simple and reflective of a child's intent and to sign in meaningful ways that preserve the integrity of the ASL lexicon. In this way, it is possible for the signing to serve as a feedback system for children—creating understandable and reproducible language that will assist them in internalizing written English, which they must do to become readers.

Let's look at some examples of text interpretation from what might be a typical book used with first-graders, *Three Cheers for Hippo* by John Stadler (1987). A beautifully illustrated book with pictures that clearly reflect the meaning of the text, Hippo saves Cat, Pig, and Dog from a swamp full of alligators. Here are some selected sentences from the story and the way Maureen Collins, a Deaf first-grade teacher, chose to guide her students through them. Prior to the guided reading, Maureen established the sign she would be using for the character Hippo with her students—a one-handed fancy twirl of her right H-hand. She sat her children in front of her and placed the book on a book stand to her right.

Picture: Hippo in front seat of airplane steering the plane; Pig, Dog, and Cat in back seat.

Text: Hippo flies the plane.

Guided Reading: Maureen pointed to the word *Hippo* with her left hand and simultaneously signed her sign for Hippo with her right hand. As she pointed to the word *flies*, she signed DRIVE-PLANE and pointed out how Hippo was driving the airplane in the picture. Pointing to *the plane,* she signed AIRPLANE.

Maureen chose the more meaningful sign DRIVE-PLANE to interpret the word flies and chose to eliminate the word the.

Picture: Pig, Dog, and Cat jumping through the air.

Text: They jump.

Guided Reading: With her left hand, Maureen pointed to the word *They* while she simultaneously signed THE-THREE-OF-THEM on the picture of the three animals. She pointed to the word *jump*, then used both hands to perform the sign JUMP, alternating hands.

Maureen performed the pronoun sign on the picture and modulated the sign JUMP to mimic the way the animals might have jumped from the airplane.

Picture: Pig, Dog, and Cat are parachuting through the air.

Text: The chutes open.

Guided Reading: Maureen bypassed the word *The* and swept her finger across the two words *chutes open* as she signed OPEN-PARACHUTE.

Rather than indicating the words *chutes* and *open* separately, Maureen swept across the words while signing their combined meaning in ASL. She then backed this up by performing the sign on the pictured open parachutes.

What we learn from these few examples is that meaning is the deciding factor in sign choice (DRIVE-PLANE versus FLY-PLANE), that pronoun signs can be performed directly on pictured characters, that signs modulate to convey meaning as depicted in corresponding pictures (the sign JUMP performed with alternating hands), and that words and signs do not have to correspond one-to-one (OPEN-PARACHUTE). These are all ways in which the morphology of ASL can be enlisted to assist children in making meaning out of print. Support for the child comes from the accessibility of both the pictures being referred to and the clear and meaningful sign language being used.

A more demanding guided reading task would be one where there are more lines of print per page, longer sentences, and messages that are neither necessarily pictured nor fully stated. Consider the following examples from a more difficult story appropriate for perhaps the third or fourth grade. In "A Ball of String," the first of three stories in Andrew Helfer's (1991) *Scared Stiff and Other Creepy Tales*, Brenda misses her bus stop and gets off in a desolate part of town. She bumps into an old scary-looking woman who drops a ball of string and then departs. Brenda unravels the ball of string despite warnings to the contrary. Rather than ruin the ending, I suggest you read the story for yourself to find out what was in the ball of string and if Brenda ever makes it home. Here is how a Deaf student of mine, Inna, guided her Deaf nine-year-old son, Sergey, through the beginning of the story.

Picture: A young frightened-looking girl is left standing alone on a desolate street near a bus stop sign. Way off in the distance is a school bus travelling away from the girl.

Text: Every day Brenda would read a book during the bus ride home from school. One day the book she read was so interesting that she missed her stop.

Guided Reading: (Although Inna did not point at each word, Sergey was watching both the text and Inna's signing at the same time.)

EVERY-DAY PT [to girl in picture] w-d READ BOOK DURING BUS RIDE HOME FROM SCHOOL//ONE-DAY BOOK PT [to girl in picture] READ w-s

wide eyes

INTERESTING PT [to girl in picture] MISS STOP//

Inna followed the text closely but eliminated articles and the words *so*, *that*, and *her*. She then signed the following in ASL: ADDITION (Explicitness): She forgot to get off at her bus stop. She was so fascinated with the book that she got off at the wrong stop.

Much like what John did when he was reading aloud to his two children (see pp. 54–59), Inna also left the text to add a more explicit explanation to ensure that the more English-like transliteration was understood.

In the next example, Inna re-signed the text in ASL, backing–up her more English-like signing with a more meaningful interpretation.

Picture: Brenda bumping into an old scary-looking woman in tattered clothing as she turns a corner.

Text: Then she heard footsteps around a corner.

Guided Reading: THEN GIRL HEAR WALK AROUND CORNER

RE-SIGNING IN ASL: CORNER PT [to picture of corner]/ AROUND [corner in picture]/ GIRL HEAR WALK

In this final example, Inna incorporated ASL pronominal reference into her interpretation through the use of indexing. The picture is the same as in the previous example.

Text: She hoped she would find someone who could show her the way home.

Guided Reading: GIRL HOPE PT [to girl in picture] FIND PERSON

PT [to space where PERSON was signed] CAN SHOW GIRL WAY HOME

The relative pronoun *who* was signed as a POINT referenced to the space where PERSON was signed just before it.

My initial thinking about this data was that there did not appear to be a hard-and-fast rule with respect to what words get signed which way. In the first example, Inna used points to interpret *she*, but later in Example 3, interpreted *she* twice through use of the sign GIRL. In the first example, she spelled w-d for the word *would* but dropped it altogether in the third example. In the first example, she dropped the word *her*, but signed GIRL for *her* in the third example. A closer look, however, does reveal some regularity in these and Maureen's examples: Words that did not have discrete signs were either spelled or dropped, and pronoun referents were either pointed to in the picture, referenced in the air, or signed by substituting their noun equivalent. In other words, there was flexibility in the ways that words were interpreted.

Let's increase the difficulty level of the text and see how text interpretation plays out at the college level. Guided reading at the college level, you ask? Absolutely. Of course, we are not talking about guiding Deaf college students through every line of all texts, but we are talking about guiding them through aspects of texts that are problematic for them. In a class situation, an overhead projector is a must—as it should be in earlier grades once print size becomes small and more lines of print appear on each page. Selected pages need to be Xeroxed and then made into transparencies that are flashed on a wall or screen. Scanning text onto a computer and then projecting it via an overhead also works. Teachers need to stand preferably to the left side of the projected text (facing the class) so that text is not covered by arms or body as it is interpreted from left to right.

One would think that the use of an overhead projector and such fundamental practices of teaching reading to Deaf students are well known, but the fact of the matter is that none of my students have ever been taught reading in this crucially important way. La Bue (1995) writes of a teacher "Anne" struggling to teach reading without students actually reading.

> Anne strived to create a natural environment for reading and improving her students' reading skills. It seemed to me, however, that she did not make the distinction between the students' understanding of a story that was told to them and their understanding of one that they had read themselves. In effect, she gave them credit for understanding her signing, not for understanding information they gleaned from the written story, yet believed this was reading comprehension. (p. 179) . . . the retelling of the story became primary and the written text secondary. Anne talked about the text. As a result, she invited the students into the world of the story rather than the world of the text. (p. 191)

I am convinced that this is the kind of reading teaching about reading that my students experienced most of their school lives simply because their teachers were unaware that students must be pulled into the text-meaning connection. This is best accomplished through the visual projection of text and meaningful text interpretation in close proximity.

One of my students' all-time favorite books is Mark Mathabane's (1986) *Kaffir Boy*, which is the story of the author's life growing up in apartheid South Africa during the 1960s and 70s. I select books with only one criterion in mind: My students must find them interesting. If they don't, they will not learn to love reading and become lifelong readers—my ultimate goal as their reading teacher. Chapter 16 begins with Mark and his father's return from a visit to the tribal reserve or homeland where his father grew up. Having read fifteen chapters into the book, my students were familiar with the traditional lifestyles and religious beliefs of the African people inhabiting the reserves, as vividly described by Mathabane. After having attempted Chapter 16 on their own for homework, they asked me to help them with the first paragraph because they weren't quite sure why Mark and his father were with the neighbors. The paragraph was projected on the wall; I started interpreting the second sentence from the book because the first one gave them no problem.

Text: On the day that my father and I returned from the tribal reserve, my mother gave birth to a baby girl, my third sister. In keeping with tribal tradition, she and the baby remained in seclusion for about two weeks, and for that period my father, George, and I had to be housed by neighbors, for the presence of males was forbidden during seclusion.

If I transliterated the second sentence, my students would not have understood it much better than having read it because it is very long, there is no support from pictures, several ideas are expressed, and the word *seclusion* was foreign to them. In addition, the reason for the separation of males and females is only offered at the end after an intervening sentence. In short, it is a much more complex sentence than the first one and not atypical of what students confront when they read texts at the college level. I find the best procedure, when a sentence is long and complicated, is to interpret the sentence into ASL first and then go back to show by pointing how the words and signs relate, or to give the students time to read it silently themselves. For this particular sentence, I read ahead and chose to juxtapose the mother and baby's seclusion with the reason for it. Here is one of many possible interpretations:

rhet-q   t

Interpretation: t-r-i-b-a-l GOD ORDER WHAT / MOTHER BABY GIRL/

rhet-q

TWO-WEEKS MUST LIVE HOME ALONE WHAT-FOR/ t-r-i-b-a-l GOD ORDER

neg

MAN++ BOY++ SEE MOTHER BABY CAN'T/ TWO-WEEKS MUST SEPARATE//

<pre>
                        t   rhet-q
</pre>
FATHER MARK GEORGE LIVE WHERE/PT [rt]   THREE-OF-THEM
NEIGHBOR WITH// MOTHER BABY MAYBE TWO-MORE SISTER LIVE
HOME PT [lt]/ SEPARATE

Note that in addition to using ASL grammatical features (i.e.,
rhetorical questions, topic indicators, negation for emphasis, redu-
plication, and setting up locations in space), I used the idea that the
tradition was an order from the tribal gods, that male members of
the family could not see or look at the mother and baby, and that
perhaps Mark's other two sisters were with the mother and baby as
well. I made these interpretation choices to create as visual and,
thereby, as clear an image or scene as possible so that my students
could picture the reason for the tradition and see the actual separation of Mark, his brother, and father from his mother and sisters,
rather than just being told about it. Once interpreted, once the students better understood the reason for seclusion, I went back to the
text and stayed with it more closely, guiding the students through
it, as follows. Having understood the meaning, their next task was
to see how this meaning was represented in English.

Guided Reading: I swept my finger across *in keeping with* and signed
KEEP, then t-r-i-b-a-l TRADITION. For *she*, I signed MOTHER, then AND
BABY STAY. As I swept my finger across *in seclusion*, I signed ALONE,
then *for about* I signed APPROXIMATELY, then TWO-WEEKS. As I swept
my finger across *and for*, I signed DURING, then signed THAT over the text
words *two weeks*, followed by the signs TIME MY FATHER GEORGE ME
HAVE-TO LIVE WITH NEIGHBOR. For the word *for*, I signed BECAUSE,
and for the words *the presence of* I signed THERE, then MAN. For *was forbidden during seclusion*, I signed FORBID DURING WOMAN TIME
ALONE. Then I pointed back to the text where it read, *she and the baby
remained in seclusion for about two weeks.*

As text becomes longer and more difficult, a good ASL interpretation sets the stage for a closer guided interpretation of it. The
interpretation reflects many of the same principles exemplified by
Maureen and Inna: Sign selection is more meaning-based than cita-
tion-form–based, as in the interpretation of the word *for* as
BECAUSE; noun referents can be substituted for pronouns, and
words signed one way at the beginning of a text need not be signed
that way throughout. As seen previously, the interpretation of *seclusion* was done once as ALONE and the next time as WOMAN TIME
ALONE, the latter incorporating more of the contextual meaning of
the term, which had accrued from the onset of the sentence. What I
added to this interpretation was a referring back, via pointing to
prior text, to more tightly connect the last mention of *seclusion* with

its first mention to reinforce the fact that Mr. Mathabane was referring to the two-week period.

Again, it is the complexity of the text that determines the need
to stay close to it or ASL interpret first or even second, as seen in
the example of Inna (p.66). The more complicated the text, the more
need to read ahead, ASL interpret, then backtrack to bring the interpretation closer to the text. Having students reread the segment
silently after seeing it interpreted will assist them in making meaning from the text directly.

Consider the next two sentences that follow the sentences from
Kaffir Boy:

Text: The day the baby was born, I spied, in the dead of night, midwives,
under a cloak of great secrecy, digging small holes near the house. When I
asked what the holes were for, I was told that "sacred things from my mother and the new child" were being buried to prevent witches from taking
possession of the stuff and using it to affect the well-being of both.

The first sentence is straightforward and can be interpreted
closely, stopping to explain *dead of night, midwives,* and *cloak of
secrecy*. The second sentence would come alive more if the
teacher/interpreter stepped into the position of the author to ask
about the holes, then into a different position to become the midwives to answer the question. *Sacred things* would need to be
explained through example, but the sentence is not necessarily
complex or unwieldy. As the teacher guides the students through
this second sentence, she can stop at *stuff* and point back to *sacred
things,* then leave the text to discuss the notion of voodoo, which is
the subtext of the sentence. The point is that teacher/interpreters
have the flexibility to stop whenever they see a need to explain,
reformulate, or add to text. Through experience, they will start to feel
when text needs to be explained, reformulated or added to, or when
a meaningful interpretation can be accomplished staying close to the
text. These decisions, however, necessitate that teacher/interpreters
read ahead to judge the nature of approaching text so that meaningful interpretation choices can be made.

The sole purpose of text interpretation is to assist students in
making meaning out of text. However, some educators of Deaf students believe that another purpose of text interpretation is to show
students syntactical differences between Sign and written text—to
contrast structural components of both languages during the teaching of reading. The goal is to make it clear to students that they are
working with two very different languages (Mahshie, 1995).

The rationale for this goal stems from thinking that written
English, or Swedish, as described in Mahshie, are second languages

for American and Swedish Deaf students respectively, and that they need to be learned *through* ASL or Swedish Sign Language, respectively. When students are learning how to read, however, they are focused on meaning and not form. It is only after students have discovered meaning that grammar instruction makes any sense. Such instruction has no place during reading lessons when students are engrossed in and actively seeking meaning. The enjoyment they experience while reading should not be disturbed by inconsequential contrastive grammar lessons that do not teach reading, the grammar of Sign, or the grammar of English or Swedish. Students can begin to acquire a feel for the grammar of text by rereading it themselves after meaningful text-Sign connections have been made. Schreiber (1980) wrote that the experience of reading and then rereading helps inexperienced readers develop a "feel" for the phrasing that is needed to make sense out of syntactic patterns. This, of course, is not the only way to learn grammar; we address other ways when the teaching of writing is discussed in the next chapter. But knowing grammatical differences between Sign and written English will not assist students in becoming competent readers. What will assist them is immersion in text interpretation until they have had enough reading practice to understand text independently.

Bear in mind, however, that many Deaf students at the beginning stages of learning to read will not become readers by simply watching an ASL interpretation of complex text and then being told to read it. This is much too magical. Deaf students need to be pulled into text. They need to see the Sign/text connection up close—they need to be taught to read. As they gain competence as readers, less pulling-in will be necessary and students will be reading in English directly. But to let beginners struggle with initial connections on their own will not support them in their quest to become better readers.

Facilitative Contexts

Appropriate texts and meaningful interpretation are the key components of a successful reading program for Deaf students, but they are not the sole components. Interpreted appropriate texts are part of larger contexts for reading that offer students opportunities to become better readers. These contexts are called "facilitative" because they are based on teaching practices that support and nurture inexperienced readers. They are indispensable contexts if understandings, ASL, and English are to be acquired reciprocally.

In the earlier grades. In the earlier grades, part and parcel of guided reading lessons are opportunities for children to read along in Sign with the teacher. This is called *choral reading*. After the teacher has guided the children through a book and the children have had a chance to talk about their favorite part or participate in a retelling of it by going through the pictures one at a time, they join in for a rereading of the story. No one is put on the spot to read alone and all children participate as best they can. When the teacher feels that most of the students are recognizing most of the words, she might consider using Post-it notes to cover words in sentences that are easily predictable from the picture on a page and then asking children to guess what word is covered. They should be shown how to use the story line thus far, the pictured page, and the subsequent picture to guess the covered word (Lynch 1986).

What is crucially important next is for the children to have their own copies of the book being taught so they can reread it either by themselves or with a partner in a *paired reading* context. Less-experienced readers are paired with more-experienced readers to continue choral reading at their own pace. Do not be concerned if at this time students only label objects in pictures, or recognize only one word out of all the words on a given page, or even tell the story instead of reading it. Such behaviors are early literacy behaviors (Ewoldt 1990), soon to be replaced by word-for-Sign/fingerspelled word equivalences signaling a different level of understanding about what the act of reading requires. During this individual or paired reading time, have videotapes of other guided readings available for children to view (the Sign equivalent of books on tape), or let them peruse books at their level independently or with their reading partner. Allow the children to take home books that they are well versed in so they can read them to family members. It would be wonderful if videotapes of guided reading sessions could go home with accompanying books so that parents could learn Sign and assist children with learning to read. Because books at this stage are clearly pictured and simple, it is unlikely that non-English–speaking parents would have difficulty.

The role that practice plays in learning to read cannot be emphasized enough. Glenda Bissex (1980) said that she sees ". . . practice being as crucial for reading success as for playing basketball or piano or any other skill" (p. 170); her reference is to practice both reading new material and rereading material. Children can tell when they are reading books better than they did previously; at the beginning of learning anything new, these signs of progress build confidence and encourage young readers to keep reading. Rereading also assists with the proper phrasing of words. As children become more familiar with the words on a page, the more they will become expressive with word groups as opposed to allotting even stress for individual words. Rereading should also not be thought of as something that only "slower progress" children do. Bissex noted that her son Paul, a fluent and early reader, chose to reread favorite books over and over again. It is a good feeling to have control over whatever is being learned.

At this early stage of reading development, a host of interactional activities assist children in recognizing words (see Andrews and Gonzales 1992 for some suggested activities), but I especially like to use dialogue journals to peak the curiosity of students. I usually start with a simple captioned picture that reveals some semiprivate aspect of my life—a picture of something special that I own or a place that I visited—and guide the students in reading the caption. When it is their turn to make an entry, they draw a picture from their private lives and caption it as best they can or with requested spelling assistance. We are not looking for students to learn to caption as teachers do, only to enjoy an exchange of meaning through a motivating reading and writing activity (all children like to learn about the lives of their teachers) that builds word-recognition vocabularies.

Extension activities based on books read should serve to enable children to use whatever they liked or remembered from a story in a different way—the hallmark of a genuine learning experience. For very young readers, art- or drama-related responses work particularly well. Children should be allowed to re-create aspects of stories that, for some reason, made an impact on them. The learning that transpires will primarily come from the doing of the activity; the more that children actively follow up with what inspired them from a book experience, the more they will remember that inspiration.

In the middle grades. As children progress through the early grades and begin to develop some language and reading fluency, participating in collaborative "talk" greatly facilitates learning to read. David Schleper (1996) wrote of the benefits of literature study circles with middle-school–aged students. Such students, with lots of modelling and practice, can start to share thoughts about what is read to deepen their understandings and simultaneously garner more practice as language users. At this stage, the continued importance of guided-reading experiences cannot be overstated. Although it most likely will be unnecessary to interpret every page of text for middle-grade readers, it will be necessary to guide students through more challenging sections.

To get inexperienced readers used to the idea of reflecting on or responding to text, they need to see the process firsthand. Teachers need to walk students through their thinking as they interpret text in Sign. As ideas or questions about what is read are formulated in teachers' minds, they should be expressed outright so that students can catch a glimpse of the hidden conversation between text and reader that reading entails.

Let's see what this might look like at about the fourth- or fifth-grade level with the beginning excerpt from the first chapter of Louis Sachar's (1993) *Marvin Redpost: Is He a Girl?* There would be no pre-teaching of vocabulary and just a passing comment regarding the picture of Marvin on the cover of the book gazing into a mirror and seeing a girl's face instead of his own. On the right are my thoughts; on the left, the story excerpt:

Casey Happleton said, "If you kiss yourself on the elbow, you'll turn into a girl."	I'm not sure if Casey is a girl or a boy here. What an odd thing to say.
Marvin Redpost looked at her.	Oh, I see. It's a conversation between a girl (because of the *her*) and Marvin. They sit together in school. Mrs. North must be the teacher
They sat next to each other in Mrs. North's class.	
Casey had a ponytail that stuck out of the side of her head, instead of the back.	Casey sounds like she's a fun kind of kid. The ponytail proves she's a girl. (Maybe not!)
"It's true," said Casey. "If a boy kisses his elbow, he'll turn into a girl. And if a girl kisses her elbow, she'll turn into a boy."	How is it possible to kiss your own elbow? Let me try to do it. I can't reach. It's probably impossible.
"Can you change back?" asked Marvin.	I had the same question.
"Sure," said Casey. "You just have to kiss your elbow again."	Like an on-and-off switch.
Marvin thought about it. But he wasn't about to try.	No, but I bet he'll try later.
At least not in front of Casey.	
"Does it matter which elbow you kiss?" he asked.	Good question.
"Either one," said Casey. "But it has to be on the outside, where it is hard. Not the soft part on the inside."	That's even harder than the inside part!

"Have you ever kissed your
elbow?" Marvin asked her.

"No!" she exclaimed. "What do   I guess she's not curious to
you think I am—some kind of   find out what it's like. I
weirdo?"   would want to do it just to
                                       see if it worked—as long as I
                                       knew I could change back.

Marvin shrugged. He did think
Casey Happleton was weird.

"Who's jabbering?" asked Mrs.   I was wondering when the
North. "Marvin and Casey?"   teacher would say something
                                       about their talking.

Marvin turned red. Everyone   I remember thinking boys were
was looking at him and Casey.   creepy when I was little. I
He hoped no one thought he   wonder why young boys and girls
liked her.   think so negatively of each other.

When we ask students to respond or react to text, we are asking them to let us in on their thinking about what they read—what
they like and dislike, what they are confused about, what they
wonder about, what they are reminded of, what they agree and disagree with, how they would handle a particular character's plight.
These are the kinds of thoughts that we should encourage students
to share in reading-response groups where they can "listen" to the
responses of their peers and use them to revamp or extend their
understandings. Rather than predesigned questions prepared by
teachers, students tackle the text from their differing perspectives,
bringing to it reactions that reflect their individual abilities and
background experiences. As Mayher (1990) points out, no one has
to play the teacher in these groups because learners pool their
resources in more of a discussion than question-answer format. As
students listen to the reactions of their peers, they will begin to
take issue with what is said or ask for further clarification, which
will require referring back to the text, rereading and, simultaneously, better reading and deeper understandings for both question-
ers and defenders.

For inexperienced readers, response (at the outset) will most
likely be self-generated questions as to what specific words mean.
Having students determine their own difficulty with a text is a very
encouraging beginning—being able to recognize problematic
aspects of text means that students know what they don't know and
that they are aware of a breakdown in meaning. Asking questions
about what words mean during response makes sense because a

framework within which to house these words is created through a discussion of the happenings in a story. This framework or context provides appropriate "cushioning" for learning new words because when these words are subsequently encountered in other settings, the context will provide the necessary perceptual and emotional hook from which the meaning of the words will be remembered.

Another benefit of response to literature is the opportunities it provides students to use the vocabulary of the text. Because most discussion will be student-led, students can see how their peers incorporate new meanings in their talk. Peer-talk can serve as effective bridges to more sophisticated use of language because new meanings are used in familiar, more understandable ways. Bear in mind, however, that as important as new vocabulary learning is for the teaching of reading to Deaf students, the reason for reading is not word learning. Rather, it is the opportunity to learn new ideas and, perhaps more important, to feel different ways. In Sachar's book cited, Marvin Redpost imagines that he has become a girl and gets to view his world from a female perspective for a day. This opportunity changes him and, in the end, makes him a more understanding young man toward young women. The rivalry between young boys and girls is well known among nine- and ten-year-old children. When students discuss what Marvin learned by being a young woman and how they feel about it (through meaningful Sign, facilitated by a teacher), their new thinking, and the more complicated language that will evolve to express it, will be the embodiment of good reading instruction.

When students become used to responding to literature, they should be encouraged to do so on their own in writing. Clear guidelines as to what is expected, along with sample written responses, will assist them as they begin this process. Some teachers make nightly entries in their own response journals and share them with their students. Marjorie Hancock (1993) offers guidelines for literature response journals with suggested ways that teachers can extend student response. She advocates teachers writing their reactions to students' responses in their journals. While this is a common procedure, for inexperienced readers it is important that response not remain totally private between teacher and student. Students should be encouraged to share their written reactions with their classmates and receive response from both classmates and teacher immediately thereafter. In this way, students gain multiple perspectives on their thinking and perhaps come to see things from different vantage points. Working alone and writing entries in literature journals during school time does not foster a free-flowing exchange of ideas among peers in which readers tackling new and challenging text need to participate. Response can be accomplished more productively if entries are attempted at home and then discussed in response groups during school hours once students are comfortable with the procedure.

Beginning written responses work particularly well in the form of personal letters between students and characters. Here, a fifth-grade Deaf student at The Maryland School for the Deaf writes to Felicity, the main character in the *Meet Felicity* series by Valerie Tripp (1991a and 1991b).

> Dear Felicity,
>
> Your are very clever when you escaped to meet Penny [a horse] every morning. I will never think of that! I thought that it was funny when your mother yelled at you about your dirty petticoats, but luckly you saved yourself by saying that you were in the garden! I would do the same thing as what you did. Are you going to ride Penny when she completely trusts you? You are so lucky that Penny ate apples from your hands! One time I went to a farm and saw a black horse, I went to it and pet it, it bit my shirt and ate it, now it has a hole in it. I am almost like you, because almost everynight, I always sneak into my friend's room.
>
> Your friend,
> Shirley

Most any reader of Shirley's letter should be able to sense the personal enjoyment she is experiencing writing to a "friend," sharing how much alike they are and the excitement of deceit. How Shirley wished that black horse ate apples out of her hand instead of leaving her with a shirt ridden with holes. These are the kinds of images that students need to recall and share with one another for, in so doing, they discover who they are and what matters to them—perhaps the best reasons for our students to become readers.

Students who are just starting out as readers at about eleven or twelve years old always pose particularly challenging problems for teachers. It is unfortunate that books appropriate for students who are just learning to read are geared toward the interests and concerns of young children. Although there are publishing companies that have turned their attention to the older beginning reader, what have been published are primarily books written at particular grade levels; as such, they are more concerned with sentence length and vocabulary control than in telling a good story the way experienced writers do. They tend to be insipid and rather flat, although certain series are more engaging than others. (See Appendix B for a listing of these series and the companies that publish them.) These stories can be interpreted and then interpreted a little at a time, after which students should be asked to reread them.

Before these series are attempted, however, students who are eleven or older, and who have no experience as readers, might focus on language-experience work as a beginning way to build up written-word recognition. Suggested activities include transcribing brief, self-generated stories that students either "tell" or act out for their classmates after they are as fully formed as possible through signed response and questioning. Students should be encouraged to reread these stories several times. Illustrating them so that they can serve as reading material for peers (and younger readers) will make the students feel like real authors, but the underlying goal is to have the students read and reread each other's stories so that written words start to become familiar.

There are also rather sophisticated wordless picture books (see Appendix C) that can be told in Sign and then transcribed, simply, picture by picture. Transcripts of these books can be compiled and reread. Simple dialogue journals styled after those described on page 73 work well with older audiences, bearing in mind that illustrations and accompanying text should reflect the interests and concerns of a more mature student audience.

The goal, however, is to move older beginning readers away from specialized readers and language experience and into the world of "real books" as soon as possible. With limited reading abilities, there is nothing wrong with selecting authentic texts that are challenging but not overwhelming. How interesting a book is for a middle-grade audience must be kept at center stage because this, along with text interpretation strategies, will assist in carrying inexperienced readers through the reading. Books such as *Journey to Jo'Burg* by Beverley Naidoo (1986) or selections from the Scholastic Biography Series slowly build context, as well as intrigue, as they move along and, therefore, do not require complex networks of background knowledge to be understood. In addition, language is straightforward and personal.

Comicbooks are another genre about which to think seriously. With speech bubbles that assist in showing who is saying what to whom and, occasionally, explicit time references in little squares, older beginning readers will enjoy and greatly benefit from guided text interpretation in small doses. Don't overlook the possibility of using the edited writing of older, more capable peers as material for less-experienced readers. The work of older students always has a spellbinding effect on younger students, both in terms of its topic, which is usually age-appropriately appealing, and its way of showing what someday these younger students can be writing when more practice is garnered.

For adult inexperienced readers. Adult inexperienced readers need accessible texts that embrace more sophisticated topics of interest. Too often, college-level developmental reading courses use selections from anthologies of essays as the backbone of their curriculum. Although there is a time and place for such materials, novels and short stories selected according to the interests of a particular group of students will be more supportive of reading growth. These genres allow readers to become familiar with characters, adding a dimension of constancy as they read. Plots slowly build from page to page providing the reader supportive contexts that a different essay or excerpt from a book a day will not. As characters and plot become more familiar, tackling new ideas (as expressed in new words) becomes easier. Again, it is the idea of a "cushiony context" of familiarity upon which to make new meaning, along with guided text interpretation, that will assist adult inexperienced readers in reading real books. Suggestions for authentic and accessible texts to be used with an adult population are listed in Appendix D. They are books that either were or could be successfully used with a diverse group of inexperienced adult readers primarily due to, first and foremost, the emotional appeal and thought-provoking value of their content and, second, the clarity of their prose.

At LaGuardia Community College, adult inexperienced readers are provided as much time as they need to read a particular assignment and write a "response paper" to it because most reading is assigned as homework. Response papers are brief, written gists or summaries of what the assigned reading was about, typically one page long. In addition, students write one- or two-paragraph–long reactions where they share their thinking on aspects of their reading that struck them in some way—parts that made them think either by reminding them of something, causing them to agree or disagree, or inducing some change in their feelings. Students are encouraged to include any questions that arise in their minds either before, during, or after their reading, either in their reactions or separate from them.

I make it clear to my students that when they write response papers they should consider them "first passes" or first tries at understanding the assigned text. They come to see that by listening to their classmates' response papers and participating in discussion, gaps in their own understanding of the text start to fill in. This discovery process, however, does not go far enough. Through the use of an overhead projector, students' non- or misunderstandings must be brought to the text, puzzled out and contrasted with the author's intent through text interpretation followed by a rereading of the problematic passage. Once students understand the ideas as expressed in written English, they, at times—depending on the frequency of their non- or misunderstandings—must rewrite their initial summary and reaction.

For inexperienced readers, making an initial attempt at understanding text, "reseeing" it after the benefit of class discussion and text interpretation, and finally rewriting one's new understandings are essential ingredients of a facilitative context for the teaching of reading. Most often, students readily see the cause of their non- or misunderstandings once text is interpreted, and can easily explain their initial difficulty. In the next section I suggest that these kinds of reading experiences must be ongoing and intensive.

Comprehension monitoring strategies. Pick up any journal related to the teaching of reading within the last ten years and you are bound to find some mention of *metacognition*—comprehension monitoring or thinking about what one is doing while reading (Block 1992). The idea is that when some confusion occurs while reading, it is monitored or recognized and acted upon or repaired through the use of specific strategies, such as rereading, integrating new information with old, drawing inferences, or reading on. I must admit to having been skeptical about this notion as applied to highly inexperienced readers because such readers tend not to stop and question if something makes sense; typically, much of what they read makes such little sense. Without a good deal of meaning being made as one reads, the whole piece, rather than only segments, tends to be problematic. Research has consistently shown that recognizing and repairing a breakdown in meaning while reading develops with age and proficiency in reading—good readers are more able to control their reading and verbalize how they do this than weaker readers (Baker 1985).

In a study of the reading comprehension strategies of two Deaf college-aged readers (Livingston 1991), I found that these readers did in fact use comprehension strategies; however, they were employed more efficiently by the more experienced of the two readers. While discussing difficult aspects of Greenberg's *In This Sign*, they were able to interpret, question, paraphrase, and integrate text information. The differentiating factor between the two readers, however, was the accuracy of their interpretations and paraphrases. The less-experienced reader had approximately fifteen percent more inaccurate interpretations and thirty percent more inaccurate paraphrases than the more-experienced reader. The problem stemmed from her inexperience as a reader in general and as a reader of narrative prose in particular. She was not getting the author's message not because of inferior metacognitive abilities, but because of her inability to understand assorted syntactic forms, vocabulary, phraseology, omniscient narration, flashbacks, and flash-forwards. She was being strategic, but devised messages from the text that were too much her own and not enough the author's.

I concluded the study by stating that the "findings imply that for learning to read it is important to provide *text-intensive experiences* in which students learn the workings of a variety of texts" (p. 127). These experiences need to include text interpretation, *as well as* monitoring strategies, so that students see what experienced readers do when they read and, especially, what they do when meaning is not readily apparent or rather unlikely. In addition, teachers or (even better) more able peers need to point out where problems exist with certain interpretations/paraphrases and to encourage students to rethink and discover why such interpretations might be unlikely. Consider the following example from the study. On the left is an excerpt from *In This Sign;* on the right are the stronger (Peer 2) and weaker (Peer 1) student-readers' responses to the excerpt. They were talking to one another about the excerpt they had read and responded to for homework.

> CONTEXT: A neighbor tells Margaret (the seven-year-old daughter of the two main characters in the story) that a truant officer was by looking for her.

But the Officer made no other visit . . . . Margaret decided not to tell her parents. She didn't know why she kept it from them; she was eager to go to school; she felt separated, younger, less fit for not going, but she couldn't bring herself to speak of it. For a while the fear lingered that the officer would come and hold her responsible and maybe put her in jail, where she would be beaten with paddles like those used in the school, but soon it too faded, and then the summer came and released them (89).	Peer 1 What??? Margaret in jail??? Peer 2 I think she was just imagining. She's just talking to herself. She feels afraid and maybe I'll go to jail. It's not really true.

What would work nicely here would be for Peer 2 to ask Peer 1 if it made sense for Margaret to be in jail and what in the text made her create the meaning she did. It is obvious that Peer 2 is familiar with third-person narration—and how we, the readers, are being let in on the thoughts running through Margaret's mind. Peer 2 is also most likely aware that the modal auxiliary *would* in both instances means *possible to happen in the future* and that Margaret is not in jail now, which is reiterated and made redundant by the word *maybe*. If Peer 2 could portray, through Sign, the fact that Margaret is thinking to herself about what might happen in the future as told by an omniscient narrator, and then point out and explain the words *would* and *maybe*, Peer 1 would understand the author's intent. With myriad exposure to these kinds of teaching experiences with a variety of different texts, she will be better equipped to employ comprehension strategies with more accurate results, thereby becoming a stronger, more confident reader.

Assessment of Readers

I used to dread standardized reading tests. There were always more than a few vocabulary words that stymied me and I almost always could justify choosing at least two of the multiple-choice answers. The topics I was given to read about had little if any appeal, and I invariably knew little about them. I always felt that if I had more time, I could puzzle-out the correct answers. They also made me incredibly nervous—especially when the student sitting next to me turned the page that I was only in the middle of reading. I often wondered why my ability to read was being tested on material that was so unlike anything I would ever read. (When was last time you read fifteen or sixteen discrete, de-contextualized paragraphs?) As soon as I felt as if I were getting to the "meat" of a paragraph, it would end.

I envy the students of today whose teachers put more trust in the day-to-day evidence of them developing as readers than scores obtained on standardized tests. These teachers are aware that students who do not shine on these tests may do very well as readers in other contexts, and that it is, perhaps, the invalidity of the tests, and not the incompetency of the reader, that can produce less than satisfactory scores. The invalidity of these tests, especially for Deaf readers, is underscored when one considers the plethora of background information they presuppose and the reduced and vapid contexts of the short paragraphs students are given to read. On tests such as these, there is no chance for Deaf students to show that, yes, in fact, they are readers.

Beginning Readers

Valencia and Pearson (1987) claim that the best possible assessment of students as readers occurs when teachers simply observe and interact with them as they attempt to understand real books. Often referred to as *dynamic assessment* (Campione and Brown 1985), this type of assessment describes the kind of support required to assist students in creating meaning from text, and differs little from what teachers typically observe during the course of effective reading instruction. For young readers, dynamic assessment would entail noting the quality of children's participation during guided reading lessons and subsequent follow-up activities: Can they interpret text along with the teacher? Are their guesses about words or upcoming happenings appropriate to the story line and/or pictures? What kind of reactions to the story do they express? How well do they recognize words from one context when they appear in different contexts? Do children "talk" about the story during other times of the day and do they use vocabulary from the story when they express their ideas about it? How well can they retell a story? Are few or many prompts required? Does the sequence of events follow that in the book?

For students just beginning to enjoy books, dynamic assessment would include indicators of how they handle books and the concepts about print with which they are coming to grips. Do children know that print moves from left to right and from the top of a page to the bottom? Do they know how to make the return sweep to arrive at subsequent lines of print?

As children start to read simple books on their own, some recordkeeping can note the number and kinds of books that they read without too much difficulty. Are the books becoming longer? Are the sentences becoming longer and more complex? Are children beginning to understand text that is not totally pictured? Are they beginning to read silently? Motivational behaviors are important to note as well. Do students enjoy reading time? Do their creative responses to stories show attention and effort?

For students who make slow progress with these beginning-reader acts, observational information can be collected on rereads of appropriate books or their own captioned drawings. If this also proves too difficult, repeated readings—where text is read and then immediately repeated back by the student—can be observed.

Middle-grade Readers

Middle-grade readers continue to participate in guided-reading lessons and in-process or dynamic assessment procedures continue to be essential for an understanding of how students comprehend text. Teachers can ask students to explicitly show, by using the text, how specific interpretations were made or what specific words and phrases mean. In addition, because these students are learning how to respond to text in reading-response groups, teachers have authentic firsthand opportunities to observe how students demonstrate what they know about what they have read. By observing discussion, teachers can see if students understood the point of a selection, the depth and detail with which they understood "what happened," and any inferences that they may have drawn. Through the kinds of questions that students ask, teachers can gauge levels of understanding and problematic aspects of a text for individual students.

Interesting observations of how readers make meaning from print can be discerned by asking them to read portions of text "aloud." In her descriptive studies of Deaf students reading in Sign, Carolyn Ewoldt (1981) showed that the redundancy of natural, whole language assists students in *building* meaning. One participant in one of her studies fingerspelled the word *genius* upon encountering it the first time in a story, but then signed SMART upon the second encounter several sentences later. The intervening sentences went on to explain how a baby learned to say words such as *philosophical* and *communication*. Ewoldt's point is that the reader was using the redundancy of the text message to discover the meaning of an unfamiliar term.

Such strategies are most apparent when students are given stories that they can read comfortably—not too easy and not too difficult—preferably stories that they choose themselves with which they are somewhat familiar. It is best to use either full stories or fairly lengthy portions of longer texts that have already been started and understood. Allow the student to silently read the text prior to reading it out loud; as he reads, note in particular what he does when he comes to language that could pose problems. Does he ask for help? (If so, encourage the student to guess.) Does he fingerspell it? Skip it? Reread from the beginning of the line or from a few words back to try the problematic part again? Read on for more information? Use picture cues? Substitute signs for the problematic language? (Do the signs make sense in the context? If they don't, does the student ignore them or attempt to correct them?) Note also how pronouns are dealt with. Are they signed? Fingerspelled? Pointed out in the picture? Given noun substitutes? Omitted? After enough text has been read (i.e., one picture book or several pages from a chapter book), the student should retell, as best he can, what he read. Compare the quality of the retelling in terms of completeness and accuracy with the observed strategies. Bear in mind that retellings need not be in-depth analyses of characters or laden with story detail. A simple understanding of "what happened?" in correct sequence is more than satisfactory. What patterns emerge for individual readers? Are there relationships between accurate or inaccurate retellings and specific strategies used to figure out difficult words or pronoun references?

Running records such as these (Clay 1991) reveal if students are reading for meaning (noting when something does not make sense and attempting to resolve the problem) or if they are just rotely matching words to signs. Teachers need these glimpses of how students internalize text and what they do when the going gets tough to better evaluate students' strengths and weaknesses as readers. Insights garnered from such observations provide worthwhile descriptive information that can be used to individualize reading instruction. If Johnny is fingerspelling abundantly with no evidence of problem-solving and provides an inaccurate retelling, he might need to see small sections of the text interpreted by the teacher and then immediately thereafter be asked to interpret the text on his own as a way of assisting him in seeing how Sign and print relate. If Johnny fingerspells abundantly, attempts to problem-solve problematic words, and provides an accurate retelling, he might be ready for a more difficult text.

A word of caution: If running records are to be accurate, it is crucial that the text be readable for students—at an appropriate level for them.

> This gives enough support from the familiar features of text for attention to shift to novel features of text . . . without losing the meaning. For it is the meaning which provides the context in which the word is embedded, the basis for anticipations of what comes next, and the signals of possible error that trigger a checking process. (Clay 1991, 337)

The checking process, or self-correction, cannot transpire productively within arenas that are too new and unfamiliar. When the context is within the child's control, however, checking or problem-solving "has high tutorial value for the reader" (p. 307). Barrs, Ellis, Hester, and Thomas (1988) in *The Primary Language Record* offer teachers in-depth suggestions for assessing progress in reading. I have found the section on Informal Assessment to be most helpful.

Young Adult Readers and Beyond

As students become older and more experienced readers, they are also becoming more experienced writers; a good part of evaluating readers' understanding of text can be accomplished through writing about what was read. This does not mean that in-process assessment as part of guided-reading lessons and through reader-response group discussions or descriptions of how students make meaning from text should cease. They are authentic assessment procedures and thereby valid ways of gauging how well readers comprehend what they read at any age or ability level. Rather, opportunities for alternative forms of assessment increase. One such form is the informal reading test devised by classroom teachers themselves.

Reading tests should be able to tell readers how they are doing with reading. They should require students to do the same kinds of reading tasks that they do in class, thereby reflecting the principles of reading instruction as emphasized by the teacher. If students in reader-response groups share written summaries, reactions, and self-generated questions about the texts they read, they should be asked to write summaries, reactions, and self-generated questions for reading tests. Students should not be penalized for lack of writing competence, but should be evaluated only on the extent and quality of comprehension displayed.

For those teachers who feel more comfortable asking comprehension questions, questions need to be varied to tap different kinds of control over text. At a literal level, students might simply be asked what a word or specific sentence means within the context of a text or, given a quote, who is speaking. At a more analytic level, students might be asked why characters behave in certain ways or how different parts of a text are related or how we know that something might happen. Asking students to write what they think the point of a text is or the reason an author wrote it focuses their attention on the larger purpose of a piece. Requesting an opinion about the message in a text or how the message impacts their particular lives almost always reveals additional understandings—as well as misunderstandings—from the reading.

Text that comprises reading tests should neither be chosen at whim nor according to any preconceived notion of grade level. Rather, it should either mirror topics that were thoroughly discussed in class or be a continuation of what is being read in class. In this way, students take reading tests with context under their belts. They are not being asked to learn something new from scratch, but rather to attempt to extend their thinking on topics of familiarity—topics for which they have built some vocabulary and concomitant concepts; stories from which they have come to know characters and motives.

In my college-level reading course, students read novels and expository pieces within a selected content area each term. Although I rarely use reading tests, I am asked to do so at the end of each semester to fulfill a departmental requirement. I am given the option of using a test that is used throughout the department or one that I devise myself; I always choose the latter option. Why, after devoting a semester to reading about apartheid or the lives of Deaf people or racism, would I assess them as readers on an article that addresses the advantages and disadvantages of using nuclear power as an energy source? How well would my students feel about themselves as readers if they were asked to read about nuclear power? Such testing makes little sense for hearing readers and even less sense for Deaf readers, who approach each reading task with substantially fewer resources to draw upon to make meaning out of text.

Topics for the tests I devise reflect the theme of the class. As such, for their required end-of-term test, my students have read excerpts from college texts on apartheid, opinion pieces on the education of Deaf children from *The New York Times,* and a *Newsweek* analysis of the killing of Edmund Perry—a black prep-school student from Harlem. College texts? *The New York Times? Newsweek* magazine? For developmental readers? Absolutely. At the time of the test, we have devoted at least ten weeks to intensive reading about a particular topic. This creates a rich network of understanding about the topic and the necessary framework from which to attempt a meaningful "read" of a complex, related piece. In fact, hearing college students do much better reading more difficult pieces on topics about which they have read related pieces than reading less difficult pieces on topics given to them "cold"—as most topics for reading tests are (E. Nieratka, personal communication, April 18, 1990).

Older students are better able to reflect on the progress they are making with reading than younger students—to self-assess their emerging abilities as readers—so I often interview my students at the end of a semester and ask if they feel they are better readers now than at the start of the semester. I ask them which parts of the course they found most and least helpful and which parts they liked most and least. I also share my perceptions of their strengths and weaknesses as readers. It is during these conferences that I hear the "if only" stories—if only I knew more words; if only my former teachers had interpreted text; if only the books I read had interested me. We finish the conference and I am left thinking that if my students can pinpoint so clearly what had been missing from their past histories as readers, then they know exactly what they need to do to become better at reading. As they conclude what for most will be their last formal course in reading, I am left feeling (and, of course, hoping) that it is more a beginning than an ending of their lives as readers.

Chapter Four

Becoming Better Writers

Similar Goals . . . Similar Tenets of Instruction

The basic premise of this book is that although Deaf students will come to know English through their transactions with reading and writing, this, by no means, is the sole purpose for the teaching of reading and writing. As we have been discussing, we "listen" and read to "find out." Similarly, we "talk" and write to share what we found out with a particular audience, as well as to better learn for ourselves what we are talking and writing about. If we talk, read, and write about topics we want to explore, our efforts become meaningful and thereby enjoyable. And what we find enjoyable, we tend to pursue, thereby becoming wiser about and better at those topics. This, then, is why we should be teaching writing—to assist students in becoming more competent at sharing and discovering meaning in written English and to help them gain a sense of satisfaction from their efforts. These goals are the same for hearing students as for Deaf students who may not know English as well as their hearing counterparts.

Yet the rationale for teaching writing to Deaf students traditionally has been quite the opposite. Educators of Deaf students have viewed the teaching of writing only as the teaching of English. Of course, there is no question that becoming competent writers requires developing a command of written English. However, where educators of Deaf students have been stymied is in thinking that competence in written English had to precede attempts at personal, far-from-perfect expression in writing; that the perfect sentence had to be practiced and mastered so that eventually the perfect paragraph could be written; that getting it down right was more important than getting anything down at all (Anderson, Boren, Caniglia, and Krohn 1980; Fitzgerald 1937). In essence, Deaf students were prevented from sharing and discovering their understandings by attempting real pieces of writing until competency in written English could be demonstrated at sentence and paragraph levels.

Bringing this conception of the teaching of writing more in line with research findings over the past twenty years into the composing processes of hearing children requires major reorientation (Berthoff 1981; Britton 1970; Elbow 1981; Graves 1983; Knoblauch and Brannon 1984; Mayher, Lester, and Pradl 1983). Modern composition theorists would argue that for students to learn how to write, teachers need to approach the teaching of writing with "holistic, growth-centered strategies" (Kirby and Liner 1981, 7), such as ensuring that "students move from simple, whole pieces of writing to more complex wholes; from short, personal writings to longer narratives . . . ." (p. 7). Kirby gives the example of how when his daughter started playing the guitar, she played simple songs before more complex ones, but always whole songs rather than a succession of discrete, unrelated chords. In addition, adults must suspend the expectation of technically accurate writing for novice writers. Inexperienced writers need to use whatever language they have in their head to "get it down" (feel comfortable with) before they need to "get it right" (Kirby and Liner 1981, 14). Rather than correcting my constant use of "hoyer" for foyer or "umpapas" for bananas when I was a toddler, my parents let me ride with it—and I rarely get them confused today. Getting it down and feeling comfortable, confident, and in control speaks to what Mayher et al. refer to as fluency development which, for neophyte writers, they argue, must initially precede worry about either how clear or correct (in line with standard written English) the message is to a reader.

These tenets, however, are based on years of studies with hearing students—students whose linguistic experiences are different from Deaf students'. Aside from the obvious difference that Deaf students do not hear and hearing students do, there are differences between the *quality and quantity* of linguistic experience in these two populations. The typical Deaf child born to typical hearing parents who do not Sign lives the first five years of her life essentially in a linguistic vacuum. Arriving at school, there are few gestures that are transparent enough to be understood by the child's teacher. Most are highly idiosyncratic and known only among family members. And, although there are differences between oral and written language that even hearing students must learn to write well, they tend to pale in significance when compared with the effects of what essentially amounts to linguistic (and thereby conceptual) deprivation during the first five years of life. Would the principles of modern composition theory still hold for such Deaf students?

If our goal for writing instruction is to assist students in becoming more competent at sharing and discovering meaning in written English, there seems to be little reason to delay the Deaf child's exposure to meaningful whole writing upon entrance to school. The crucial component of successful writing instruction would be to ensure that "facilitative contexts" are at hand—that Deaf children are writing to share ideas they choose to share and are given myriad opportunities to do so without the "axe of correction" held over their heads. If adult expectations of mature writing are initially suspended, there seems little reason to delay what can surely be an enjoyable experience for children, regardless of the degree of "oral" linguistic/conceptual preparedness they bring to the task. There is little doubt that a thriving language system provides the best foundation upon which to teach reading and writing. At the same time, however, "oral" language (both spoken and signed language) and written language have distinct properties that can be learned reciprocally right from the beginning—*in concert with* one another, each enriching the other—given appropriate contexts wherein writers write for their own purposes without fear of being wrong.

What follows is a developmental look at different-aged Deaf students learning to write in just such contexts. Although the emphasis is on the teaching and learning of writing, the mutual dependency of what is learned on students' abilities to Sign and read should be apparent throughout.

Facilitative Contexts for the Teaching of Writing
Early Writing Experiences

Given a print-rich environment chock full of good children's literature, where pictures and objects on display are labelled and where children's own creations (i.e., drawings and paintings) are labelled according to their own dictates (see Chapter 3, p. 63), Deaf children, as hearing children, will try their hand at making their own marks on paper. Ewoldt (1985, 1990) chronicled the development of early writing behaviors in Deaf children of both hearing and Deaf parents. Early attempts are scribbles, primarily just for the fun of the feel of them, but soon take on added dimensions of meaning when, "for example, the child may make a scribble and see that it resembles a duck. Thereafter, that scribble *is* a duck" (1990, p. 107). Further development is seen in strings of unrelated but salient letters—especially memorable due to perhaps a "tail" or a "tunnel" (Clay 1991) or because they are easy to produce, as seen in the early writing of one Deaf five-year-old in Figure 4-1. Children start to write letters in different positions and begin to see that the same letters can be rearranged to create different "looks." A stab at their own name, as shown in Figure 4-2, brings them closer to the understanding that written symbols carry important messages.

Figure 4-1

Figure 4-2

Such early attempts need to be celebrated so that children are encouraged to continue their exploration of letter formation. Those not ready (as determined by teacher judgment) can continue to dictate their intentions or form words through the use of plastic letters. The goals, however, are for the child to build a core of known words that he can both read and write independently, and for him to become acquainted with the way print works—that words are formed from left to right and that there is an intransient order for letters in a word if they want to convey its meaning appropriately. Andrews and Gonzalez (1992) offer a variety of interactive environmental print activities (e.g., writing orders from a menu, exchanging notes) that spur kindergarten Deaf children with first writing-reading experiences.

As children become more comfortable with writing, they will begin to label their own drawings (see Figure 4-3).

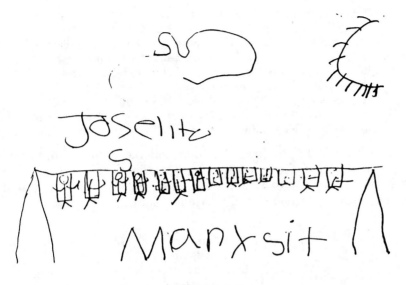

Figure 4-3

Although some teachers of hearing children at this level encourage their students to "sound out" the word, this, of course, is clearly inappropriate for Deaf children (and actually of limited help for
hearing children). Some children will remember where they last
saw the word—perhaps in a book or located on a chart in the
room—and some will attempt to spell what they remember of the
word. This should be encouraged, although most will need the
word spelled for them. Writing the word down for them or having a
more able student-speller assist are other means of exposing children to print at perhaps the most meaningful time—when they need
it. It has been my experience that writing words on paper or the
blackboard rather than fingerspelling them out creates a more lasting visual image by enabling children to capitalize on the spatial
attributes of the printed pattern. It also results in fewer requests for
repeats of the spelling.

From here, the importance of exposure to accessible children's
literature (see Chapter 3, p. 51) cannot be emphasized enough, for it
appears to be the driving force in both Deaf and hearing children's
writing development. It is not uncommon for Deaf children to retell,
in writing—according to their own level of understanding—a story
that has just been read to them. In fact, this appears to be the next
growth indicator after picture labelling. Having been exposed to
myriad storybooks, children begin to understand the idea of
sequence, yet still (at the outset) need the support of someone else's
ideas for their own rendition.

CONTEXT: Billy, a profoundly Deaf six-year-old boy, had just been read Joan Nodset's (1988) *Who Took the Farmer's Hat?* As the story goes, the wind blows a farmer's hat off and the farmer goes from animal to animal asking if "anyone" has seen it. Each animal responds that it hasn't, but in the same breath says that it did see something. So, as examples, the mouse sees a hole in the ground, the fly sees a round brown hill, and the goat sees a flower pot. In the end, the farmer finds his hat in a tree being used as a nest for some birds. He decides to leave it there for them.

The teacher distributed paper and pencils to the children and requested that they draw or write anything they would like to about the book. Billy did not refer back to the book again. He required some spelling assistance but also used a picture dictionary.

> corn cow
> farmer hat stands
> ran away farmer hat
> tree bird baby four
> Farmer see nothing
> Mouse like brown hat
> squirell like brown hat
> tree see branch climbs
> see bird Nest baby four
> see hat new
> can house

Billy's teacher was in ecstasy with this piece and with just cause —it was one of his first attempts at sustained writing. She asked about a "next step" with it—as many teachers do—but decided instead to display it, to call the principal in to see it and, most importantly, to revel in Billy's accomplishment. Nothing else. Our goal was fluency development—to keep this writer writing where-in, perhaps, a new piece of writing might be in the offing.

Children soon begin writing about their own experiences, recording what they recently did or what recently happened in their lives. Most often they relate experiences on class trips or at home, as in the following example:

CONTEXT: Fred, an eight-year-old, hard-of-hearing boy, wrote about a trip to my house. All eight children waited in the school bus while I bought pizza. My husband (Peter) arrived home. Some of the children jumped on the bed; others watched *The Price is Right* and ate chocolate ice cream.

The children wanted to share their experiences at their teacher's house with their schoolmates. We thought the best way would be to compile their writings into a booklet for distribution.

Sue house

1 Sue my* house.
2 bus we eight stay Sue walk pizza.
3 come Peter home
4 house and Janie came a Peter
5 Luis yesterday absent Wednesday
6 bed Gary and Armando play fight
7 ice cream and brown chocolate
8 home school
9 home bus school
10 t.v. Armando car win   yes   no **

---

* her or Sue's
** if he were a contestant on *The Price is Right*

Although the side numbering might be a vestige from former experiences with tests and language workbooks, I think it was more an aid in helping Fred to recall the events in the order they took place. I was amused to see a very snappy ending to a rather typical kind of language-experience exercise, and noted as well his inclusion of a title, indicating perhaps that Fred was paying attention to beginnings and endings in his reading work. Fred's piece was distributed to his school friends as is.

CONTEXT: Janie, an eight-year-old, profoundly Deaf girl, ran into the classroom signing very animatedly about her brother. To ensure that her message was being conveyed, she tried her hand at writing it.

Pedro Bolivar
school p.s
class 185R
teacher Fresh
Pedro Bolivar Bad
telephone 843-1971
mother angry Pedro
Father go home
Father angry *Pedro*
belt Father
mother say" Father

What is particularly exciting about this piece is that it reveals the beginnings of narrative structure. We see a bit of character development, intrigue or conflict, and a glimpse at resolution. (Although readers probably wonder what mother told father.) In addition, new incidents ". . .develop out of the most recent addition rather than turning to the constant center" (Applebee 1978, 69) because every part of the story is necessary and adds to its point (however rudimentary). Because this piece was Janie's first attempt at story generation, and because her goal was still to develop a feeling of comfort with writing, her work was celebrated with her classmates and posted on a bulletin board outside the room.

But if stories such as this one are not spontaneously generated by young Deaf children, how do they learn to write them? My daughter's early attempts at writing stories were her renditions of books that had been read to her. Sometimes she created the exact story line with different characters and different objects; sometimes it was the element of surprise that intrigued her that eventually appeared in her own made-up stories; other times it was a particular form—dialogue—that drew her attention and carried over into her own writing. Books that engage children serve as powerful models for them and appear to be helpful, if not necessary, as grist for their own writing mill, as any reading material is for writers of all ages. After all, our ideas do piggyback off the ideas of others.

It is nothing less than tragic, however, that too many Deaf children of hearing parents arrive at school without ever having been read to (or ever having been told stories). We have already discussed the implications this has for learning to read in Chapter 3, but because reading and writing are so intimately related, children who have not been read to are at a disadvantage in learning how to write as well. Without familiarity with how stories work (i.e., characters experiencing conflict and working out resolutions), it is difficult to know how to write them. Without the myriad understandings that reading aloud offers, it is difficult to find topics about which to write. Plainly put, without their knowing what a story is, it means little to say to a class, "Write a story."

Given plenty of opportunities in school to see stories told, to read and be read to, Deaf students will, over time, begin to internalize the concept of story. In addition, it will be particularly helpful if they can participate in the construction of a story or observe first-hand how a story is written. This is what we did in one class with Jessie, an eight-year-old, hard-of-hearing girl.

Context: The morning read-aloud selection was Rosemary Wells' (1992) *Hazel's Amazing Mother.* Hazel's mother sends Hazel off to purchase some food for an upcoming picnic. Hazel gets lost and runs into a band of troublemakers who destroy her toy doll and carriage. Just at that exact moment, Hazel's mother has a premonition that something is wrong with Hazel. Amazingly, she arrives on the scene to save Hazel from further torture and makes the band of no-goods fix Hazel's doll and carriage.

After reviewing and discussing the story in depth, the teacher shared a simply written, simply illustrated (with stick-figure drawings) self-created story mirroring the theme of *Hazel's Amazing Mother:* A mother sends her child off to the park on her bicycle; the child is accosted by a group of older children who demand that she turn over her bike to them; the mother gets wind of this and saves the day. At each turn of the page, students were encouraged to share what they thought the next page would be about. The children were then given their own blank books and asked to draw and write their own stories. Brief "idea conferences" were held with those students who experienced difficulty thinking of a story. Here is Jessie's:

Jessie's Mother

> Jessie's Mother gives money.
> Mother says, Buy "food."
> Jessie is sad because the girl takes the money.
> Mother Amazing.
> Mother says, "Stop."
> Mother gives the money to Jessie's.
> The End

The beginnings of story generation, then, appear to take root after exposure to stories in school. It is not uncommon, however, for this understanding to slowly develop, for it seems to require not just passing exposure but sustained exposure to the workings of stories. Although story generation was attempted with a group of six-year-olds who had been in school for two years, the result was more isolated picture-labelling than story production. This merely means that these children need both intense exposure to accessible stories and time for their linguistic/cognitive system to become "story-ready." *Jessie's Mother*, then, was indeed a coup for Jessie and she was proud to share it with the other children on her grade level who had been read the same story.

Billy, Fred, Janie, and Jessie will become more fluent writers as time progresses if they continue to be immersed in enjoyable and purposeful reading and writing activities. Understandings gleaned from their readings will be reflected in their signing and writing. To correct or have the children rewrite any portion of these pieces would be disheartening for them and pedagogically inappropriate at this point. They are still only at the very beginning stages of written English acquisition; their initial attempts should be celebrated and, most importantly, respected.

Other genres of writing might also be tried with young children. At The National Center for the Study of Writing and Literacy, researchers are studying how hearing six- and seven-year-olds write stories to persuade their classmates to play with them, as well as stories for their classmates to act out—how they are using writing as a tool to accomplish their social desires. The researchers call this kind of writing curriculum "permeable"—where instead of mimicking the kind of writing that teachers may value, students' ideas about the kind of writing they want to do permeate the daily lessons. Students, Deaf or hearing, who are fortunate enough to be in classes where teachers seize "teaching moments" from students' leads, will reap the rewards of being both more socially sophisticated and more persuasive writers (Dyson 1995).

The Beginnings of Response and Revision

As children become older and are exposed to more reading and writing, some of their writing becomes both longer and more complex. Such growth, however, does not necessarily mean that pieces will be easier to understand. At this stage, it is helpful for writers to see the effect their pieces have on an audience—most often through the response or feedback of their peers and teachers. The purpose is to show the writer where his meaning is not fully or accurately conveyed, as well as to extend the writer's thinking on his topic by offering different perspectives and insights. Students begin to understand that first attempts at writing a particular piece are not permanent—that they can be made clearer based on reactions they receive from their peers and teachers. Students, however, need to be eased into these notions and require lots of practice with both giving and receiving response.

By ten or eleven years old, most Deaf students feel comfortable writing personal experience stories or fictional narratives. Topics usually stem from their life experiences, but they are also ideas encountered in books they have or have been read. I especially like to share slightly older Deaf students' writing, as well as the writing of similarly aged hearing students, to "prime their writing pumps." For neophyte Deaf readers, the writing of their peers (especially personal or fictional narrative), seems to spellbind them because they are usually about topics with specific appeal to similarly aged students. I also find that student writing offers students appropriate "scaffolding"—the ideas expressed are within their frames of reference and the language used is in advance of but not inaccessible to most. Students' journals also offer a wealth of possible ideas for writing topics. Teachers, who typically know their students inside and out, might consider jotting down possible topics for particular students as they come to mind.

Together, with the students gathered around (most often) the blackboard, we begin to either read a particular piece of peer writing or watch a particular picture book being read aloud. If the students will be reading a particular piece of writing, the reading should be visually displayed and interpreted (as described in Chapter 3) to ensure that the intent of the piece is conveyed, as well as to afford additional exposure to written conventions and vocabulary to which students implicitly pay attention. Picture books should be selected with care, the best ones have engaging, clearly pictured story lines that invite students to delve into further discussion.

What follows then is a lot of "talk." First, we talk about what we just read or saw—what it was about. (We can't go much farther until this is accomplished.) Then we talk about whatever the piece made us think about. We begin to meander inside our own territories and find similarities and/or differences between what the author wrote about and what has happened in our own lives. We talk about what we liked or didn't like about the piece; how it made us feel. We ask questions about ideas or language we didn't understand. As the students participate in this exchange, they encounter their classmates' ideas, which trigger more of their own ideas. As each idea is brought forth, it is written down on the blackboard so that at the end of this "brainstorming" session, students who still feel in need of topics to write about have something to which to refer. Interestingly, however, it has been my experience that these "getting-started-writing activities" have only some impact on the topics students eventually select. Typically, students write about something they just wanted to write about.

During writing time, everyone writes. Children will ask for spelling assistance and should be encouraged to use picture dictionaries, books, or journals where they think the word might appear or to ask more spelling-able peers. Schleper (1992) suggests ways of keeping students writing, although they may have difficulty spelling, by either writing what they think the first letter of the word is, drawing a line where they get stuck, trying it and circling it, drawing the picture, or even drawing the sign. I do not think it wrong, however, if teachers provide spelling assistance; logistically, it works well if she is positioned in the middle of a desk grouping with Post-its or index cards where words can be recorded, given to the student in need, and later entered into a permanent word file for that child. In addition to spelling assistance, students will request help in translating their Sign meanings into written English phrases and sentences; this assistance should also be readily given in written form.

When students feel that their pieces (finished or not) are ready to be shared, and if this is their first exposure to response, it is helpful if the teacher tapes her piece on the board first and the teacher's assistant models response to it (or vice versa). This response should be no different than that used in responding to reading selections in general where students tell what a piece is about, react to it, and ask questions. In essence, we participate in a conversation about the piece with the writer.

In one fourth-grade class, the teacher wrote of her decision to give her dog away. It was becoming too tough for her as a single parent to care for the dog in a New York City apartment. Her decision was made after arriving home from work one day to find that the dog had soiled her bed. After her story was taped on the board and Sign-interpreted, the class discussed what the story was about and related stories about their pets.

At that point, I asked the teacher about the effect her decision had on her children and what the new owners were like. I also wanted to know if hamsters or a guinea pig might be in the stars as next pets. As a class, we felt that these additions would make the teacher's story "better" and more fleshed out. We composed these additions on separate strips of paper and taped them next to the lines in her story where we thought they might make the most sense. For homework, the teacher was to revise her piece as we demonstrated.

Using the teacher's piece first enabled the children to see that even her story needed to be modified to fit her listeners needs and that, yes, even the teacher's story had to be rewritten. This served several purposes. It concretized the understandings that the class was "all in this together," and that no one's writing, Deaf or hearing, is perfect the first time. In addition, there was no child singled out first for what might be perceived as negative criticism without a run-through of the process beforehand. Finally, it clearly showed that a first draft was only a practice draft, which subsequently made the children more accepting of "mess" on the first go-around and the garbage pail considerably less filled with crumpled papers that weren't "neat."

Nicki wanted to share her story next. It was taped on the board and she Sign-interpreted it for her classmates. This was her story:

> My father climb my housetop
> My father XXXX said
> Nicki come papi year*
> wait what up.
> Then climb my house
> on stand Then me
> almost fall My father

said Don't fell
Nicki said o.k.
Chimney broken cut
the bricks on the chimney
My father said please
help.
Nicki said O.K.
Nicki, My father I XXXX fix
My father said I wand to
fix house.
My father said clean
house now
Nicki said O.K. I clean
Yes house
Nicki said can who help
people come is help 6
My father said O.K.
Oh My god I please
No O.K. Look. tomorrow.

---

* here

During writing time, Nicki needed to know the words for *bricks* and *chimney* and the phrase *cut the bricks on the chimney*. She completed this first draft in about thirty minutes. When she shared it with her classmates, we applauded her efforts and gave the following meaning back to her.

> Nicki's father asked Nicki to help him cut some bricks on their chimney. Nicki agreed but almost fell standing on top of the roof.

It was difficult for us to go much farther with the piece for, as Nicki saw, we were having difficulty understanding the italicized portion about *people* and *6*. Nicki, upset by this, explained that while she and her father were fixing the chimney, six other people saw them and asked her father if he would fix their chimneys as well. He agreed to look at their homes the next day. As a class, we composed the following on a strip of paper:

> Six people saw my father fixing the chimney and asked, "Can you fix our chimneys too?"

Had Nicki reacted differently to the class' response, I might have directed their attention to her use of the word *clean* because I was not totally clear about her intentions there as well. However, this was Nicki's first time experiencing response and the whole idea of redoing writing. Her reaction to the response told me that one clarification was enough at this time.

Although there were other possibilities for the translation of her intention about the six people, I chose to introduce the use of quotations because a quick review of her writing—eight uses of the word *said*—suggested that she was ready to learn how to use that element. She was also most likely coming across direct address in the stories she was reading and picking up on its use. We asked Nicki to rewrite the second page of her story to include the revision we modelled in class; that was as far as we decided to take this piece. On a different day we could go back and take a look at the *clean* word choice, as well as other instances where quotation marks would add clarity to the piece.

Maria's writing posed different concerns. During writing time, Maria kept referring to her journal where she had started to write an entry about a friend, Liz. She was using her journal as a dictionary to help her spell the words she needed.

> *My Mother* XXXX weird Liz said No
> change Ha. Ha. Ha. Me Maria kill stupid
> kill No please stop hate Liz
> shut up Liz sorry hate much
> yells Dreams stop o.k.

Although the class knew that Liz was a friend of Maria's, they had too many questions about the piece to talk about what it was about. Most problematic was knowing if Maria killed someone and who hated Liz. The class also needed to know if Maria dreamed she killed someone and how her mother was involved. Seeing that her classmates genuinely wanted to have answers to these questions made Maria eager to answer them and, as I sensed, eager to know how to write them so that she, too, could have a story. We decided to ask Nicki to work with Maria during the next writing time so that a second draft could be prepared and shared with the class. Nicki sensed what Maria needed to know—to be more explicit with her subjects and objects—and together the girls created Draft 2, the final draft.

> I Bad dream.
> I woke up time 12:00 night
> I woke up afraid
> Me yells.
> because why Liz. Kill me

Until Maria develops more fluency with writing, grammatical concerns should be put on hold.

The goal of early response to writing, then, is clarification of meaning, but subsumed under this goal are various factors that must be considered. Determinations as to how many requests for clarification are too many for beginning writers must be made with the feelings of the writer in mind because the notion "my writing, myself" embodies much truth. Think about how familiar the student is with receiving and sharing response. Is the student comfortable with his classmates in response-group settings and fairly confident in himself as a writer? Consider also the purpose of the piece. Is it going beyond the confines of the classroom? If a lot of attention is given to correctness, how much of a piece will end up being written by the student? Because students often need assistance in phrasing their revisions, we certainly do not want our language to consume much of the piece. If a particular piece is to be valued by the writer, it must be the writer's, there is little pride in a piece that ends up being barely yours. With practice, teachers will learn how best to respond to and require revisions of a particular student based on the needs of that student and the purposes of a particular piece.

Consider Juan, whose story about a hermit crab was written and illustrated without assistance after having read *Is This a House for Hermit Crab?* by Megan McDonald (1990). In the story, a hermit crab goes scritch-scratching along the beach in pursuit of a new shell-home. Some shells are too big, some too little, but the perfect one is eventually found. Spaces between text indicate separate pages with corresponding illustrations. Juan was not familiar with giving or receiving response.

Hermit Crab beach
by: Juan

The Hermit was very
very hungry.
The hermit get slow.
The hermit have
scritch scratch.
Hemet make sound. walk.

Hermit crab under the wood.
Hermit crab came out of
shell. Hermit got bigger.
crab look for New house.

Hermit find a small shell.
Hemit can go in shell.
the crab is stuck. in shell.
crab don't like ti. Hemit move out
of shell.

Hermit eat fish and drink water.
Hermit eat too much food.
Hermit got fat. Hermit feel
Good be fat. Hermit find bottle on
beach.

Hemit fall in the beach.
hemit Leg are hurt.
Hemit go to the doctor.
Man Give to the bandgae.

Hemit feel better.
Hemit go home.
Mother ware Happy and Mother
Give present. Hemit say what in the
box. Mother say open Now.
Mother say in the shell.

Hemit crad surprise and Hemit open
the box. Hemit change house and
Hemit have Now home.
The End

If I were responding to this piece, this is the kind of conversation I would have with Juan about it:

Hermit Crab finally got his house! He got bigger and couldn't fit into a small shell. He fell and hurt his leg and had to go see a doctor. After he felt better, he went home and was surprised to see that his mom had bought him a new shell for a house.

What a clever ending!! Moms seem to know everything, don't they? I'm glad Hermit has a proper-fitting house—I can't imagine walking around with clothes or shoes that are too tight!

Did Hermit get bigger because he ate too much? I'd like to hear more about that bottle—is it what caused Hermit to fall? Was he trying to get into that also?

If Hermit got bigger because he ate too much, Juan would need to do some reordering of sentences to establish this information first or to use the conjunction *because* in between getting big and eating too much. Helping his audience about the bottle would require him to add a few more story details. Reordering and adding are typical revisions that all writers do when they reread their piece or receive response from a reader; Juan, as a writer, will need to learn how to do them.

A question here is how to handle correctness issues. In light of the questions posed, I would think that, because his writing is fairly fluent and there is some control over beginning written English, Juan could learn how the use of pronouns and the consistent spelling of Hermit would make his story more like "book language" and a real book that perhaps younger schoolmates would like to read.

As students progress through middle school, learning how to be competent responders to writing is a crucial goal. Naturally, we want Deaf students to become better writers, but as circular as this may appear, students will learn what clear writing demands by being able to respond well to writing—to articulate what a piece of writing is about, to react to it, and to formulate genuine questions about it. However, the Catch-22 is that Deaf students need to read well enough to note when events in a story do not make sense, or when language is non-understandable, or when the point is not clear in order for them to respond well. Here, perhaps more clearly than anywhere, we see the symbiotic relationship between one's ability to read and one's ability to write. One cannot be a good writer unless one is a good reader—a reader who probes for meaning and asks relevant questions when meaning is not being totally or clearly conveyed. One cannot be a good reader unless one is a good writer—a writer who internalizes these strategies when composing her own writing. As flip sides of the same coin, then, responding well to writing and writing well are virtually inseparable.

Later Response and Revision
at LaGuardia Community College

As Deaf students become more practiced readers, writers, and responders, they will be better able to work independently in response groups. The goal is for students to offer their peers quality or helpful response—response that deals with issues of clarity that impact a peer's second draft. Hasty responses such as "Good" or "I liked it" or "Everything's fine" or "You need to write more" are not very helpful. Similarly, asking one or two superficial questions that do not penetrate to the heart of a piece doesn't give the writer any direction to follow.

A good way, I find, to improve as well as monitor response quality is to require that all responses to a peer's first draft be written. Not only do I see firsthand what has happened in a group, but because the response must be written, it becomes more thoughtful and carefully done primarily because it demands a slow read and rereads of a particular piece. When group discussion begins, there is "meat" to discuss; when the work is finished, the writer gets a written record with which to leave the group. The responder, in turn, gets additional practice with writing and I get a clear indication of how well he is reading.

Perhaps the most important benefit of response is that students soon realize that when the tables are turned and their writing is being responded to, they will want to write in ways that make it easy for their peers to understand their intent—so that fewer questions are asked of them. Students begin to understand that as they compose, they need to "hear" the voices of their peers asking questions about their points, or what this or that means. This monitoring needs to be made second nature to students so that an ongoing internal dialogue is established as they write. It is this internal dialogue, or reflection on their writing as they write, that is prerequisite for students to become better at writing.

To assist my students in selecting topics of their own to write about, I offer them essays that are alive with messages targeted for an adult audience so that students' opinions and feelings can fly during discussion. For students (or anyone, for that matter) to write well, chords of desire with something to say need to be struck. Such writing, however, must also be accessible to students who are not yet skilled readers, as well as helpful in offering students ways of organizing their own writing. (See Appendix E for a list of suggested essays and collections of writing that can serve as model essays.) Because of this, I like to use excellent peer writing that I have anthologized over the years (*Voices of Deaf Student Writers: 20 Top Stories*—see Appendix E) and distributed to schools for Deaf students not only to show them examples of excellent writing that they can comfortably read and analyze, but also to inspire them to become published authors themselves. In the jargon of the language -development field, excellent peer writing is appropriately "scaffolded" to accommodate the needs of less-skilled writers.

Students read an essay or group of essays for homework and bring their written responses to class. Other than the fact that it is written, it differs little from the kind of response we have been discussing: I ask for a brief gist or summary of the readings, a reaction to it, and any questions that come to mind either before, during, or after the reading. I start class by focusing on the students' reactions to what they have read. By the end of class, we have usually arrived at an understanding of a particular piece's gist and have discussed most of the students' questions. Time is also devoted for an in-depth look at the structure of the published piece, where we note particularly effective leads, patterns of development, and conclusions.

After class discussion, students begin to think about a particular notion that struck them—something that the readings made them remember or what they found particularly interesting about which they might want to think more. They are given time to write their initial thoughts in the form of notes, lists, free-writing, or questions. Students may work alone or with peers to prime their pumps before a first draft is attempted, but before they leave class, they "talk" through their thinking on a possible topic with me. I rarely require specific forms of writing (i.e., narrative or expository), but rather work with students to create the necessary form that best expresses what they have chosen to write about. However, students, are exposed to different genres in both their assigned readings and anthologies of student writing and, typically, by the end of a twelve-week session, they have tried their hand at an assortment of genres for their ten required pieces without formal directives.

Students compose their first drafts, unpressured, at home on what we affectionately call "magic paper"—paper that simultaneously creates three copies of whatever is written. (It can be purchased from Standard Forms, Inc., 6800 Jericho Turnpike, Syosset, New York 11791.) Magic paper is also lined and numbered, which makes it helpful in referring to specific language—we can say, "page 2, line 6" as opposed to referring vaguely to "toward the top of page 2" or having to tediously count lines. Students skip lines and leave a large left-hand margin so that their responders can jot down the point of each paragraph as they read them. This enables the student/responder to see the flow of ideas more clearly, making it easier to note where points appear from nowhere or where they "derail." Of course, students can generate first drafts on a computer, but they are responsible for bringing three copies of their work to class with lines numbered. On a separate sheet of paper, responders then write a brief summary, reaction, and any questions.

Following is a first-draft piece written by Gilberto, a student in a developmental writing class for Deaf students at LaGuardia. The class had just finished reading and responding to *On Being 17, Bright and Unable to Read*, a short, autobiographical essay by David Raymond (1989) who poignantly depicts what it was like to be a learning-disabled high-school student. After discussing the essay, students were free to choose any topic to write about, but class discussion focused on upsetting experiences during their own school careers; topics for essays naturally followed. Here is Gilberto's first draft:

When I was 9 year old. I was so innocent child. My school deaf had influenced me. There were many deaf students in small room and they almost XXXX didn't use the sign Language. They just talked by Lips. The staffs was hearing and strict. my director too. I really remembered that my group of my class was fun and best XXXX classmates.

Early morning, I was XXXX so excited to get up quickly. My mind starve to go to school. My Father picked me up to school, seeing me how happy I was. We arrived at there, dropping me. I entered in greeting all deaf students who knew me.

When we was in class, I sat at a square table with deaf students. One of deaf student talked creative with sign. I saw him signing odd!. so that I couldn't copy it. So He taught me how to signing and I didn't know what it meant. It seemed that is fun!!! I tried to practice that sign. Finally, I make it and I had it To remind.

After that, when I finished the class, I was so excited that my father will pick me up to my home. I still bother my mind that sign was so great!

Other morning, My Father and my mother was wearing the clothes, I Told them that I wanted to show my odd sign to them, Suddenly, they was so shocked, I didn't know what had happened. My mother hit my hands. She told me that it was sin and God can punish me. They was worried that who influenced that to me. However, I didn't know what my odd sign Language meant and I thought that this sign meant airplane. It was wonderful sign.

After that, I met my deaf Friend. I told him what had happened about my parents. They laughed histeraly!! so that the one of them taught me what the sign mean. Finally, I was disgusted to know what it mean.

Wow, I have a great remember when I first learn the bad sign., but it is Funny to my parents scaring. Now, I had never forgetten this story. I hope that deaf children shouldn't influence again to students as me. . .

Below are Laura's and Phil's written responses to Gilberto's draft. Laura's written response was:

Summary. When he was 9 years old and an innocent. He attended to Deaf school and his deaf friend who influence to him for new sign language. But that school was very strict and not allow to use the sign language. Every morning he always excited to attended that school because his have deaf friends. One of his deaf taught him by signing. And he came home and show his mother that he did signed it but his mother hited his hand and said "Sin and God". He got confused and went to school told his deaf friend that what happened. His friends was laughed so hard. Now he got it what mean and disgusted and his knew it. He had a great remembered when he learns a lot of sign language but know what's mean bad things sign.

Reaction. I don't blame you. I was happened about this, when my friend who know speaking spanish language and taught me a spanish word. I did it learn that one and went home that I spoke with it. When my mother heard it and said it to me that "It's not nice in the house and don't ever say it again!" I was shocked of my self and don't understand why. Next day, I told my friend about what happened this situation. It was so laughted and said it me that *"It's curse word!" Now, I know it, oh well I think, it was an experience but joking.*

Questions. *What's signing mean? is it bad or disgusted?* Your parent were accept that you learn sign language with your deaf friend? is it worth that you can feel free deaf friends communicate than your parent are speaking with reading lips?

Phil's written response was:

Summary: Gilberto is great. He never trouble in school. He was good boy. Gilberto's parent happy. Gilberto was his friend and influenced sign language. He like to sign language but Staff demanded lipread all student. Gilberto's father always pick-up him at school. He was very interestine sign language his hand. Gilberto. Gilberto was his mother angry him. She was shocked him. He wanted to show sign language front of mother. She asked, "sin and God." He never do again. Gilberto was great.

Reaction: I was interestine about a story life. Gilberto really wanted to learn sign language early year than late year. He was good's friend. I felt that Have right to sign language. The classmate not allow sign language. Staff decided not like sign lauguage much better Lipread. My obey

Questions: How get up morning during School Where is from school deaf or mixed Hard of Hearing? Why father anxious Gilberto was all the time sign language?

Comparing Laura's response with Phil's, it becomes clear that hers is the more helpful of the two. It seems that Phil thought the point of Gilberto's story was that Gilberto's parents were upset that he was picking up signs from his friends at an "oral" school—missing the point that it was one particularly vulgar sign that when presented to Gilberto's parents caused them to become upset. Without this knowledge or even a question about what was learned, Phil's response cannot help Gilberto, as seen in the rather innocuous reaction and the three more or less irrelevant questions that he posed. Laura's response, on the other hand, was right on target, sophisticated, and helpful. Her summary, but moreso her reaction, revealed that she understood Gilberto's point. The last two lines of her reaction (italicized) not only provided Gilberto with the phrase he needed (*curse word*) but also showed that through subsequent discussion, she might be able to take the story to a different level—that what happened to Gilberto is part of life—almost a rite of passage most students have to endure on their way to becoming older. Most important, Laura's first question would be the first one that comes to any good reader's mind—what was the sign????

During response time, Phil would see Laura's response and participate in a discussion of it, which would serve as a mini-reading lesson for him. Once aware of Gilberto's point, he most likely would have further, now on-target, reactions and questions of his own to contribute through discussion. I always respond in writing to each of my students' first drafts but hold back my response until I hear what the group has accomplished on its own. I try to stretch my students as writers in the kind of response that I offer, probing beyond the given text to delve into the significance of a particular piece—much the way Laura did on her own with Gilberto's essay. I see it as my role to ensure that students' essays leave both writers and readers "moved" in some way—that upon completion of a piece of writing, we say "Hmm" and not "So what."

What happens at this point is left up to the writer. Aware of his group members' responses, Gilberto revises his piece according to how crucial he sees their suggestions for the way he envisions his story. In addition to having copies of Laura's, Phil's, and my written responses, during discussion he has taken notes as to what revisions he will make and at what line he will make them. If I do not get a chance to sit in on the workings of a response group, I ask the writer to share his plan for the second draft with me before he revises it.

Draft 2, while typically more fleshed out and connected, is once again presented to response-group members. This time, comment focuses primarily on how Draft 2 is better than Draft 1 and what else needs to be done to make it even stronger. At this stage, discussion still centers on a student's intended meaning—if enough information has been provided to make the reader fully understand the writer's points and if the order of presentation makes sense and is as effective as possible. Attention is next paid to, first, the most problematic sentences of the piece of writing and then to the recurring grammatical concerns. During computer lab time, using two adjacent computers—one as a "blackboard" and the other with the student's essay on it—the student and I work collaboratively to rephrase, in writing, the sentences that most interfere with meaning. Following are examples of language in need of rephrasing from Gilberto's draft, which are primarily indicative of his unfamiliarity with English semantic domains. In other words, Gilberto needs to see how English allows certain combinations of words to express certain kinds of meanings and not others.

They just talked by lips.	(They just lipread each other, or They just used lipreading, or They were oral Deaf students.)
It still bothered my mind that the sign was so great!	(I was still thinking that the sign was so great!, or It still bothered me that the sign was so great!, or It was still on my mind that the sign was so great!)
In the morning, when my father and my mother getting dressed on the clothes . . .	(In the morning, when my father and my mother were getting dressed; or In the morning, when my father and mother were putting on their clothes.)

As seen, several possible interpretations are written for each
sentence and the writer records the one he prefers to use.

At this point, a student's meaning is expressed as best as possible and certain cumbersome phraseology has been interpreted into
written English. Although I make it clear that essays at this stage are
considerably more understandable, I also make it clear that outside
readers in general and the Chair of the English Department in particular (who, in consultation with me, decides whether students
move on to English Composition) will think differently of their abilities if their essays do not conform more to standard English. This
is never a hard sell. As mature students who realize that they will
soon be entering full-credit courses with hearing students, they
want their work to be as correct as possible. There is no doubt that,
at this stage of the process, my more serious students do benefit
from "plain" correction. I often see them "slow-reading" their corrected piece—studying it carefully—which, as mentioned on p. 71,
is actually an excellent way for them to internalize English. And,
yes, I do see carryover of correct word choices, some verb tenses,
and word order from one piece to another. However, correcting is
not teaching and specific grammatical instruction at this stage is
most definitely warranted. Obviously, one cannot expect to teach
Gilberto everything that he might need to know about his particular
piece at one point in time. But there is little reason not to teach him
some things. But which things?

I teach the grammatical aspects that students seem to be on the
verge of acquiring on their own and the needed grammatical knowledge for the errors that recur and interfere the most with the meaning students are trying to convey. I use each student's piece as his or
her own grammar text and, therefore, at this stage, work individually with students. My goal is to teach them the requisite editing skills
along with appropriate terminology for specific grammatical aspects
that they hopefully will be better able to control or at least correct
in the final draft of the next paper. So, working with Gilberto's draft,
I might focus on the following:

1. When I was 9 years old. I was so innocent child.

Gilberto seems to understand that introductory sections can
be separated from main sections of a sentence through the use of
a comma, as evidenced in the following constructions from his
first draft.

> Early morning, I was so excited to get up quickly. In class, I sat at
> a square table with Deaf students. After that, when I finished the
> class, I was so excited. . . . When we was in class, I sat at a square
> table. . . .Wow, I remembered when I first learned. . . .

He needs to be reminded that just as *when I finished class* and *when we was in class* do not stand alone as separate sentences, *when I was 9 years old* also cannot stand alone as a separate sentence because the reader is left wondering, "What happened when you were nine years old?" The first part of the sentence, called a *dependent clause*, needs the second sentence, *I was so innocent child*, the independent clause, so that we know what he was like at nine years old, just as we know that when he finished class, he was so excited that his father was picking him up, and that when he was in class he sat at a square table. I would also explain that when this dependent clause is used as a full sentence, it is called a *fragment*. Encountering this error in subsequent essays, I would call Gilberto's attention to it through correction symbols, but expect him to know how to correct it himself.

> 2. One of deaf students talked creative with sign
> I saw him signing odd so that I couldn't copy it.

Here Gilberto would need to know that *creative* and *odd* function as adverbs, which tell us how verbs are done—how a Deaf student talked and how he signed—and usually end in *ly*. It is not necessary at this point to explain that they describe adjectives and other adverbs.

It is important to note that the grammar teaching I do in these contexts does not depend on the grammar of ASL. When I teach grammar, ASL is the language in which I teach, but I do not contrast the grammatical principles on which I am focusing with their expression in ASL. The errors Gilberto made were based on his conception of how written English works. He must be shown how written English works to express himself. He does not need to compare how dependent clauses are used in ASL with the way they are used in written English, nor the way ASL modifies signs to incorporate additional meaning while English uses adverbs. He was in my class to learn how to write, not to become a comparative linguist.

How long does grammar teaching take? Fifteen minutes tops. I could hold four individual conferences in a sixty-minute period, which means that approximately half of the class could be attended to in one period—often during a computer period when students are busy revising drafts, affording me much-needed undisturbed time. The beauty of working with students one-on-one on grammatical issues is that the instruction hits home with them. There is a purpose for them to learn these elements because they need them to make a particular piece better—a piece that will be shared with the class as a whole; a piece that will be part of their semester's record.

It is important to them and, therefore, the instruction sticks with them. As Otte (1991) states:

> I am convinced that what any one of my students needed in order to develop the requisite editing skills was something at once considerably more focused and considerably more complex than anything I could find in any textbook—and believe me I looked. The students' patterns of error and blindspots in error recognition had a kind of individually circumscribed specificity and at the same time a causal intricacy that made going after them with any of the available textbooks like going after shrimp with a tuna net. Even class time spent with the students' own writing was best spent as general limited preparation for more individualized and intensive work in one-on-one conferences. (83)

Although I agree with Professor Otte about individualized and intensive work on students' own essays, I do use grammar books as reference and practice books for my students. I suggest exercises based on the kinds of errors that appear in their writing (e.g., Gilberto would be assigned extra practice with correcting fragments and using adverbs). I also devote the first fifteen or twenty minutes of two class periods per week to aspects of grammar that befuddle all my students. They seem exceptionally appreciative of the opportunity to repeat on their own as homework the grammatical principles they learn in class. These lessons help them understand not only the structure of English, but also (when I conference with them individually) what I mean when I ask, "Does this verb agree with its subject?" or "Would you like to use direct or indirect address here?"

There is no doubt that grammar teaching is important. But what is perhaps more important is knowing the time and place for it within the context of a writing program that seeks to develop and sustain students who write to share and discover their ideas and gain satisfaction from doing so.

Assessment

Former New York City Mayor Ed Koch made a point of asking—perhaps too frequently—"How'm I doin'?" Although he professed to need a sense of how he was doing his job, he knew exactly how he was doing without having to ask, simply by reflecting upon his pre-election promises—his goals and expectations—in light of his post-election record of accomplishments. Come Election Day, when it was time for his constituency to make a final determination of how he was doing, at each of two re-election years, I am sure there were no surprises for him.

We all like to know how we're doing, but we, too, can answer that question for ourselves, as long as we know what we have to do, and if we can judge whether if what we did was successful based on a set of standards that we understand and accept. While it is up to teachers to assist students in the actual doing of writing, if the assistance is effective, students will, over time, be able to judge for themselves their successful pieces, and to articulate why these pieces were successful. These decisions need to be based on criteria that guide them throughout the term and with which they, become thoroughly familiar.

Becoming familiar with criteria for good writing, however, presupposes much exposure to reading and writing, as well as to much talk about what good writing is and plenty of samples. To begin this dialogue with young Deaf children would be inappropriate, but for it to be embedded in the writing curriculum for older students would not. Teachers and parents of young Deaf children, however, would still need to clearly understand how their children are doing with writing.

Assessment of Early Writing

Early writing ranges from scribbles to emerging stories in free-writing contexts. Little is formally taught but much is celebrated and learned. Evaluation at this stage would be descriptions, perhaps over three- or four-month periods, of what the children are attempting. The following categories might be helpful:

Fluency Development

- Scribbles
- Randomly connected letters
- Words
- "Sentences" (intended but perhaps not fully grammatical)
  - number of "sentences"
  - number of words per "sentence"

Varieties of Writing Attempted

- Labels for drawings
- Lists
- Letters/notes
- Dialogue journal entries
- Written responses to readings
- Poems

- Stories
  - rewriting of an already told/read story
  - personal experience stories
  - fictional story or different version of an already told/read story
- Scripts
- Persuasive notes

Emerging Forms/Principles

- Beginning to leave space between words
- Periods
- Capitals
- Quotation marks
- Pronouns
- Increasing awareness of how words are spelled

Strengths as a Writer

- Shows interest in writing
- Writes frequently
- Readily selects topics
- Makes use of a personal word file
- Writes for longer periods

These categories are not meant to reflect the definitive word on writing assessment for young Deaf children, but are suggestive based on an accumulation of writing samples over much time. Teachers need to carefully observe and document the kinds of growth in writing that they see happening in their classrooms and to share these growth indicators with colleagues and parents. I kept a pad on my desk to jot down brief dated anecdotals on particular children as they occur (see following example); the note goes into the child's writing folder at the end of the day.

Jimmy

10/92 – First try at using periods.

12/92 – Word *said* appears after seeing it many times in his reading.

These kinds of notes can serve as a much-needed database for research into the development of writing over time in young Deaf children; classroom teacher/researchers have the best vantage point. The notes also provide a running record of growth that can be shared with students, administrators, and parents.

Assessment of More Fluent Writing

As children grow older and if they have been continually provided myriad opportunities to read and write, the longer and more story-like their writing becomes. At this point, students are participating in writing conferences, learning how to respond to each other's writing, and how to revise a piece. In addition, because they are more experienced readers and writers, they are becoming more aware of and comfortable with written English and are ready to learn more about its structure. Assessment of writing ability, given this context, needs to speak to the evaluation of all these components, as in the following suggestions:

Fluency Development

- Are first drafts becoming longer?
- Are sentences within first drafts becoming longer?

Variety of Writing Attempted

- Personal narratives
- Fictional narratives
- Autobiography
- Letters/notes
- Dialogue journal entries
- Written responses to readings
- Poems
- Mini-reports (Guided—see Chapter 5, pp. 142–145)
- Scripts
- Persuasive pieces

Response Quality

- How well does the student articulate what a peer's piece is about?
- How in-depth and helpful are the student's reactions? (Are new ideas generated for the writer?)
- How important to the piece are the student's questions?

Revision Follow-through

- How carefully did the student revise his work?

Emerging Forms

- Which aspects of English structure and/or conventions of written English were worked on?
- Is there increasing awareness of how words are spelled?

Strengths as a Writer

- Shows interest in writing
- Readily selects topics
- Writes pieces of interest to his peers
- Experiments with engaging leads (beginnings) and satisfying endings
- Adds humor to a piece
- Tries out dialogue
- Describes what characters look and/or act like
- Begins to reread and reflect on work
- Writes for longer periods

Response quality and revision follow-through need to be discussed and noted as soon as possible after students have had opportunities to respond and revise. These discussions should pinpoint for students how their reactions or questions helped a particular writer and how certain revisions made pieces more understandable.

At three- or four-month intervals, students should be able to sit down with their teachers, select two or three of their best pieces, and discuss why they selected them based on some of the criteria suggested under *Strengths as a Writer.* This could include any other criteria that you and your students may have created together based on models of excellent student writing to which they have been exposed (see p. 98). They might also want to look for pieces that were particularly hard for them to write or ones that they just didn't like. In end-of-term conferences, teachers and students can reflect on students' selections to document how far students have come and where they would like to go with their writing. Having been through the assessment process many times up to this point, they should have little difficulty articulating for themselves, "How am I doin'?"

Assessment of Writing in Secondary and Postsecondary Settings

At secondary and postsecondary levels, Deaf students are exposed to more sophisticated texts in a variety of genres. Through either guided reading or interpreted read-alouds, they continue to internalize the workings of more demanding writing, such as the use of time shifts, point-of-view shifts, extended description, and development of points by example. Although reading engaging works of published authors is a a good way to "fire up" students for a discussion of characteristics of effective writing, I find that showing them excellent writing examples of my former students impacts their own writing more. There is certainly a time and a place for students to see models of the craft of more intricate writing, but the pieces of effective writing that need to be carefully looked at as examples to emulate need to be within their reach.

We design our own evaluation criteria by looking at both fiction and nonfiction pieces and talking as a group about why we consider the writing to be good or not good. We typically come up with the following questions to consider when reading a piece of writing, in the order presented:

How Interesting is the Piece to Read?

- Does it have a real voice? Is it lively and natural, the way most people talk?
- Does the piece pull you in and leave you feeling different after you've read it?

Does the Piece Contain Enough Detail?

- Can the reader clearly "see" what the writer wants him to see?

Are Word Choices Appropriate, Strong, and Non-repetitive?

Does the Piece Stay on Track Without Derailing?

- Is there a logic to the way thoughts are ordered?

Again, these questions are merely suggestive and are best developed through discussion when samples of accessible writing are read and evaluated as a class. Thereafter, students begin to refer to these characteristics when discussing each other's writing in response groups. It is important that they become familiar with the vocabulary of evaluation so that at the end of a term, they can review their successful and less successful pieces and articulate the reasons for such judgments. An end-of term summative evaluation, written by the student, would further make students aware of the learnings they accomplished. Linda Rief (1992) offers some questions students might ask themselves as they compare pieces of their written work over a term.

Evaluation criteria at this level also need to include some understanding as to how students responded to one another's work, as well as the thoroughness of their revisions. I like to ask members of a response group to comment on the quality of response that they received from their response-group members. I ask them how in-depth and helpful their peers' responses were and which ones made them see their paper in a different light. This needs to be discussed and documented soon after the first meeting of a response group. How effectively students revised their work should also be addressed, most appropriately when they are talking about differences between their first and second drafts. Evaluation of response and revision quality, then, are in-process evaluations best accomplished in response-group settings by the students themselves.

Some indication of the kinds of grammatical structures and/or conventions of written English that were taught in conference with the teacher should be made. Again, it works best if students document this instruction for themselves so they can begin to articulate, and hopefully remember, specific grammatical/editing concerns they need to pay more attention to in subsequent writing. I leave room on the evaluation sheet of each essay for students to write in specific structures and conventions on which they focused for that essay.

As students become older, they are expected to become better at evaluating themselves as writers. They will get better at this by knowing, along the way, what their work is expected to be like at the end. Talking and writing about how pieces differ in quality and why is perhaps the best documentation of growth in writing for which students and teachers could ask.

Facilitative Assessment in More Formal Contexts

The fact that Deaf students' writing will be assessed by readers other than themselves and their teachers at various points in their school careers is unavoidable. City- and state-wide tests of writing ability, as well as college entrance exams and tests taken to show eligibility of movement from one level of writing ability to another, are, unfortunately, here to stay—at least for a while. It is time, however, to rethink the validity of these tests, given the contexts I have described herein, which I believe are supportive of the development and evaluation of students as writers.

At a recent workshop sponsored by the National Council of Teachers of English, an ESL-teacher at one of the branch colleges within the City University of New York distributed a piece of writing done by one of her students as a final exam. The student was given two hours to write about a topic of her choice ("The History, Pros, and Cons of Fortunetelling"). The piece of writing was to be the sole criterion for either exiting or repeating her current course—the lowest of a three-level sequence of courses for ESL students. Two outside readers both agreed that the writing did not display the abilities required for the next course (due to its lack of grammatical control) and recommended that the student repeat the course. The teacher was upset with this decision because she felt the student had come a long way during the semester, learning how to structure her essays and elaborate her points, and now was being held back by grammatical errors. To prove her point that the essay was a fluent and coherent piece of work, the teacher rewrote the student's essay, cleaning up some of the grammatical knots and thereby making it better, so she thought.

The essay was fluent and well-structured and, yes, there were grammatical problems, but after reading the corrected piece, I suggested that it was perhaps not the grammatical errors that bothered the readers as much as it was the unclear nature of several of the major ideas the writer was trying to make, for which the teacher's grammatical correction still defied elucidation. These ideas needed to be revisited through "talk." Additional information that would most likely have made the writer's intentions more accessible to readers would most likely have been requested in a peer-response –group setting; this kind of talk should have been "allowed" in the testing situation.

This is not cheating. If teachers spend time teaching response and have their students participate in response groups (which this teacher did), shouldn't this very crucial component of the writing process "count" and be included in any test of writing proficiency? As a writer, I am always seeking additional readers for my manuscripts and am amazed at how the quality of my work improves after hearing multiple perspectives. Including opportunities for students to respond to each other's writing in testing situations does not imply that the need of some writers for additional practice will be masked by the assistance given them. Once response is given, it will be up to the writer to figure out what to do with it, just as I must decide how to change my manuscripts based on the feedback of my colleagues. This is how real writing is accomplished. It is a natural part of the writing process that should not be artificially excluded from tests of writing ability—especially for inexperienced writers.

Dialogue Journals

There was something magical about Monday mornings in my writing class. I would begin the class by returning my students' dialogue journals having, responded (much to my husband's dismay) to them over the weekend. The journals contained our written conversations over the course of the term and I would watch in awe as they feverishly turned to my latest entry and read, absorbed in its content, until completion, stopping only to ask for clarification of a word meaning or two. I was convinced that if only they relished the readings I assigned in such a manner, there would be no such thing as a reading-writing lag. What was it about these journals that so intrigued them? I initially thought they were so well liked because they were substantially easier to read than other required readings. I was wrong.

I remember introducing the idea of a written exchange with my students in a rather nonchalant way. I told them that in addition to their required essays for the course, I would require letters from them about anything they chose to chat about. I purposely used the term *letters* since they already had a well-developed schema for that concept in their semantic repertoire—seemingly more organic and less abstract than "dialogue journal." I made it clear that for each letter they wrote, I would immediately write one back, and that they should feel free to ask me any questions about anything they wanted to know (within reason). This process, I explained, would continue for the duration of two quarters (twenty weeks). There was no resistance; only a why or two. My response to the whys was, "Because it will be fun for us to converse informally and will afford you additional practice with writing and reading." Those were my rather unlofty goals but, down deep, I was curious to see how they would shape this idea of letter-writing to fit their needs.

I started noticing that each student had a specific issue or issues that kept recurring in their letters. These were more than extended topic chains; they were real-life, pressing *concerns* that were placed on the drawing board, discussed, and somewhat come to terms with over several months. It appeared that my students needed a forum for this—as evident in their comments:

"What do you think about. . ."
"I want to ask you something about. . ."
"Should I . . ."

Following their lead, I wrote letters to them that mirrored exactly what I would have told them had these issues come up in face-to-face conversation. The difference, however, was that our dialoguing transpired over an extended period, which provided my students more opportunity to ponder their responses and weigh my contributions—which I sensed they needed to arrive at preliminary resolutions. Additionally, the extended time enabled them to incorporate ongoing, daily-life occurrences into their specific situations, which would have been difficult to do in any depth in the limited and sporadic time frame of student-teacher conversation. I was always there for them in writing.

In the excerpts that follow, one of my students, Fran, demonstrates how, over time, having someone to converse with whose opinion she valued assisted her in coming to terms with an issue of importance to her.

On Fran's mind was her relationship with her hearing boyfriend, Julius.

1/15
Dear Sue,

Last weekend, I dated deaf guy's Joey, he is hard-of-hearing. Last Saturday his first night to move new home. We helped each other to cleaned up all the junk boxes. We enjoyed talked our old times because we know from our old high school. We get along very well. I do treasure Julius and I don't want to lose him. Also I haven't fell love with Joey not yet. I think Joey is crazy about me. *So I guess I have take time consider whether deaf guy or hearing guys for my future. If you have any questions, feel free anything or pick on me. I like to challenge with you and also it help me to think hard why, reason, could be sometime I am wrong re of my life.*

1/16
Dear Fran,

Stop killing yourself over whether you're going to end up with a Deaf guy or a hearing guy. Just go with the flow—if you are comfortable and happy with a particular guy and have certain feelings toward him, then that's the guy for you. Only those criteria should be of concern—not whether the guy is hearing or Deaf. It's the same thing we're discussing in class regarding Black and white. You seem to fit nicely into all four worlds (Deaf, hearing, white, Black), so you have a multiplicity of combinations of guys to choose from. Don't worry so much because you will certainly know when the right one comes along. Just make sure that you can trust the guy and that he makes you feel good.

1/17
Dear Sue,

Guess what I spoke with my boyfriend Julius last night. He is very exciting to move here New York maybe around first week of February. Now it is time close wow. *It making me little nervous and exciting too.* My family tease me when Julius arrive here, you can't go out other dates. *I don't know what to do ha ha. Of course I am continue to date with deaf guys. But I don't know when Julius get here. That big difference situation.*

1/19
Dear Fran,

Oh boy . . . You're having second thoughts about Julius coming next month. This sounds pretty serious because it seems that

Julius is ready for something that you are not. You'd prefer him to stay a while longer in North Carolina to give you time to think. Why do you have to cut yourself off from dating other guys once he arrives here? It might be that he is ready to make a commitment to you. If this is the case, try to hold him off for a while until you are sure about what you want.

1/20
Dear Sue,

I have half feel excite to see Julius and other half feel I want Julius to stay South little longer. *When Julius get here I should tell him the truth how my feeling.* I know Julius does not want to have open relationship. I guess I have to wait what happen. I do treasure my guy Julius. *Now I am not give up to continue to date deaf guys.*

2/28
Dear Sue,

Last week my boyfriend called me that he might get other job work in movie in Wilmington, N.C. again. I told him I was really mad but I have acceptance the life come first job. We spoke on the phone for a long time. I am going visit him on 18th of March. Of course I will tell him that I don't trust him anymore. My girlfriend jokes me maybe Julius finally move here until ten years. I said no way and better not happened. *My feel start begin mix up because first I am angry at him, other feel I am gave up don't trust when he decided to move here and other feel I am excited to see him two more weeks to go.* We stayed together for three years and I told him "I am mad at him but I love him." *I need your opinion if you were in my shoes will you doing break up with Peter [teacher's husband] when he is Wilmington, or you refuse to give up and believe to faith one day we will married. Or talk him one more last chance or move back to North Carolina or go head date other guys ha ha ha.I know it is not easy to be apart and to decided what to do important my life first.* Now my mind flash light that I remember last night I dreamed about all stuff above that story. Also I remember something in dream I was doubt broke up, yell mad, and something else I couldn't remember it. Of course when I get to see Julius I will kick his ___ with my shine red boots ha ha. I will tell him how I feel expression.

3/6
Dear Sue,

Yeah I agree with you "oh Boy" about Julius ha ha. I agree with you maybe Julius scared to find jobs or maybe scared make commitment to me. When I found out Julius got the job from few days ago, I am still little mad at him since to until present. So my mind start to build up to appear many things said to Julius when I visit him on 18th of March. *I can't wait to tell him last chance because I feel it not fair we are make agreement already.* Well I have to wait see what happen on my vacation in Wilmington, N.C.

3/7
Dear Fran,

Don't threaten Julius. Obviously, if he isn't coming to New York, he doesn't want to. You can't make him. Forget about your agreement—his head is in a different place now than when he made the agreement several months ago. Distance can be the worst thing for a relationship—"out of sight—out of mind."

4/6
Dear Sue,

I told Julius that I decided want to open relationship and he accept my word. Of course he don't want open relationship. Well too bad for him. Last week I wrote long letters as serious. *I am not forward wait to hear from him to move here New York.*

4/10
Dear Sue,

Julius have not decided when he will move to New York. *I pray hopeful that he will move here before Fall start. We are still relationship.* Of course, I am taking time myself, I want to enjoy myself.

5/23
Dear Sue,

Julius suppose come visit here New York by next weekend, but I don't believe. He knows I am cold person which mean I didn't want talk him at all. *I prefer Julius to be here and we will discuss our straight out should keep relationship or the end of relationship.* Other way I do still love him very much. That is why I don't want to tell Julius to broke up on phone or letter. I prefer face-to-face. No I don't guilty [about dating other guys] because I don't waste of my life.

6/1
Dear Sue,

Julius arrived here New York. We have been talked very serious about our relationship. *Julius decided to stay here. But he will continue work movie in Wilmington, N.C. which mean he will go back and forth here New York and Wilmington, N.C. Right now I am waiting to see what happen our relationship next time. I would feel better Julius stay live here N.Y. and come back work in N.C.*

6/12
Dear Sue,

Right now I treasure my boyfriend and we already that we discuss about our future. Julius is value my future life, But if other guy hit my heart then maybe I will give up Julius HAHAHAHA. Right now Julius had two home here New York and Wilmington which mean he will in and out.

For now, at least, Fran seems content with her relationship with Julius although her thinking about it took some typical twists and turns before arriving at this stage: When he was eager to see her, she started worrying about her freedom to date; when he held back, she wanted him more. As of June, the "in and out" aspect of the relationship affords Fran time to date other men and to consider just how serious she is with Julius. Although she seems to want a serious relationship with him, she still wants her freedom as well. From January to June, Fran figured out how not to commit for now.

I am quite sure that Fran discussed her concerns with other friends and family members as well. However, this was the first time that these concerns were brought up with a teacher who happened to be hearing, older than her—though not quite yet a senior citizen—as well as a woman with a relationship. Gaining this different perspective seemed of the utmost importance.

"You are older, different idea. It helped me to realize and think twice about my life in the future."

"I love to read your philosophy about anything."

"I am so glad that we can share our personality so maybe I will learn something from you."

"I wish to learn hearing's culture."

In this light, what I originally initiated as fun and to provide additional practice with reading and writing took on a drastically different dimension. Although I basically offered my opinion and raised questions that I thought my students needed to hear, these opinions and questions served to create "hearing-teacher mainstream" parameters with which they wanted to compare their thoughts and actions. They were looking for alternative and/or corroborative cultural perspectives with which to evaluate their individual plights.

Considering the linguistic vacuum that my students grew up in (i.e., born Deaf to nonsigning hearing parents), they are most surely due every ounce of feedback they could possibly garner. Letter-writing became the vehicle for this necessary feedback: It was continuous, frequent, student-directed, and quickly became student-demanded because there was payoff in it for them—they had real motivating reasons for writing and reading. Yes, it was also fun, and yes, it afforded them practice with reading and writing. But most important, it gave them the confidence they needed to come to tentative terms with issues of change on their minds. They understood themselves better after these exchanges; in this light, most pedagogical benefits pale in significance.

Not that there aren't pedagogical benefits that accrue with frequent dialogue journal-writing. They ". . .include a rich variety of the language functions essential to knowing and using a language: requesting information, complaining, evaluating, reporting personal facts, promising, speculating, arguing and persuading, warning, advising, offering opinions, and apologizing" (Staton 1985, 132). By its very nature, journal-writing creates interested readers who pick up reading in the best of all possible contexts—real-life, human-interest (if not downright gossipy), and student-directed. Journals can be the repository of a plethora of possible "more formal" writing topics and can be used with Deaf children of all ages (Staton addresses their use with six- to eight-year-old Deaf children in the source cited previously) to varying degrees and, I am sure, similar feelings of excitement. After all, isn't the idea of writing personally to your teacher a thrill at any age?

Chapter Five

Signing, Reading, and Writing to Learn in the Subject Areas

A veteran hearing teacher of Deaf students—a staunch supporter of the use of ASL—once told me that she found it rather unsettling that the bulk of exposure her middle-grade students were getting to English was only during times set aside for reading and writing classes. Although she embraced the notions of her bilingual curriculum, she felt that her students were being shortchanged on English. Interacting all day and, for the majority of her students who lived in dorms, all evening, in ASL left little time for interaction in English.

Students need to be inundated with text, to be immersed in ideas as represented in meaningful words, *in all subject areas* to learn English, thereby becoming bilingual in the true sense of the word. This is perhaps easier said than done considering that the typical content-area class is forty-five minutes long. Using ASL as the primary language of instruction, by the time topics are introduced and discussed, where is the time for reading and writing? Content-area teachers may perhaps see responsibility for reading and writing as solely that of the language-arts teachers. However, actively reading and writing at only set times during the course of a school day will not provide students—Deaf or hearing—with enough practice time to become competent and confident readers and writers. More important, *language arts teachers do not own reading and writing*; reserving the teaching of reading and writing for them artificially separates language processes that work best reciprocally when "juicy" topics of interest are being studied. If the major theoretical thrust of this book is that signing, reading, and writing develop best while students are learning, and that language and learning cannot be teased apart, it makes sense for subject-area teachers to be afforded more time to incorporate reading and writing more wholeheartedly into their instruction and, likewise, for language arts teachers to connect and expand upon these new learnings by offering related readings and writings.

This reciprocal notion of learning subject matter through reading and writing is not new. Often referred to as "writing to learn" or "writing across the curriculum," its basic premise is that as we read and write to learn, we simultaneously get better at reading, writing, and learning. What is intriguing, however, is the idea that it is particularly the act of writing that enables us to think more clearly about the ideas inherent in our texts and to somehow more permanently anchor them in our memory. As we write about what we are learning or write to express what we think we have learned or know, we (at various times) tend to solidify our thinking, recognize how much we don't know, question what we think we know, and see ideas in different lights. In this way, we come to more fully know or "discover" what we are writing about.

Of course, we do not only write to learn in the different subject areas; we observe and sign to learn as well. But there appears to be something more permanent to our learning if it transpires in contexts that require us to read, write, and sign about what we have read and written. But how might this kind of learning happen with Deaf students, who typically possess reading and writing abilities that limit learning through those modes? After all, students must be able to possess some degree of reading and writing skill if they are expected to learn through reading and writing.

The reason why reading and writing have not proved successful for the learning of subject-specific information in schools for Deaf students is due more to inappropriate ways of using reading and writing to learn than to the abilities of Deaf students. Inappropriate methodologies, however, are unfortunately not restricted to schools for Deaf students, but are characteristic of educational practices in less-enlightened schools for hearing students as well. A typical scenario is this: The teacher assigns a list of words that students must define and use in a sentence out of context—usually before students have seen the words in a text or before they have built any experiential framework into which to fit the words. The students then look up the words and copy the first or, more likely, the shortest definition; since the definitions are usually just as unmeaningful to the students as the words they are looking up, any real vocabulary learning is only remotely possible. This holds true even when vocabulary words are housed within a text, since most often the kinds of subject-specific texts students are given to read independently are beyond their grasp, precluding the possibility that context might be used to support vocabulary development. Teachers often wonder why their students can't write coherent sentences using their weekly vocabulary words. The reason is because the words do not yet belong to the students. Their meaning is still only accessible to those who have lived with them longer.

Consider the assignment: "Answer the questions at the end of the chapter"—specifically, the questions that "Focus on Key Vocabulary." Some textbooks require students to answer review questions in complete sentences using an appropriate key word from the chapter. Students are only being asked to scan the chapter for the sentence or two that contains some of the words in the question and then copy out the sentence that houses the boldfaced key word, as shown in the following example:

> **The question:** What did Ann Hutchinson do when Puritan officials ordered her not to preach? (Armento et al. 1994, 204)

> **The text:** When the colony officials ordered her to stop preaching her beliefs, Hutchinson practiced *civil disobedience.* . . . (Armento et al. 1994, 193)

Even questions that focus on reviewing concepts are of the locate-and-copy nature.

> **The question:** New England didn't produce valuable cash crops because _____.
> (Armento et   al. 1994, 204)

> **The text:** New England farmers couldn't produce cash crops like tobacco for sugar because of New England's rocky soil and cold climate. (Armento et al. 1994, 198)

This type of assignment, akin to a kind of visual-matching, search-and-seizure mission, is a far cry from anything that might remotely be considered reading or writing to learn. Students copy textbook words and textbook language with little opportunity to internalize the ideas, making them their own. The true understandings belong to the authors of the text and the teachers; the students serve merely as scribes.

When more thoughtful ways of using reading and writing to teach subject-specific information are practiced, both Deaf and hearing students will come to know more and, in so doing, will get better at reading and writing about what they know. The theoretical underpinning of such thoughtful ways of teaching is simply this: Inexperienced readers and writers must be provided with contexts that escort them along the path of new learning until they have built enough experience to wander along the path themselves. Without such support, students will just mark time and never really get to where they need to go.

Suggestions for Integrating Signing, Reading, and Writing into Subject Areas

Infuse Subject Areas with Picture Books

For novice readers and writers learning the subject areas, the wide use of pictures to clarify and enhance what is being learned cannot be advocated enough. If students are to make meaning from new ideas expressed in new language, pictures provide the necessary support through which new learning can be more easily created. Without the assistance of pictures, meaning from only text and Sign, at initial stages of learning anything new, cannot be made as clearly. Pictures can begin to level the playing field for students who have had fewer opportunities to learn in language.

Little has been written about the power of pictures to convey meaning and how crucial their use is to good teaching. My first encounter with this power was using my peripheral vision to watch my daughter as I read aloud to her from a variety of different picture books. Her eyes would first sample the pictures on each page, then zero in on something that pulled her in. She would remain transfixed at this certain something until it was time to turn the page. Pictures did more than elucidate the corresponding text; they took her to the scene through their power to kindle her imagination. There can be no better way to get a hold on what it is that needs to be learned than to see it (or do it) in conjunction with talking, reading, and writing about it.

Many informational picture books (i.e., books about specific subjects and events) are also well written because they usually are written by authors with an intense interest in the subjects. Choose well-pictured books whose pictures portray corresponding text and whose texts do not merely recount facts, but infuse stories with information in memorable ways—through a touch of conflict, an in-depth view of a character's personality, and vivid description. Quality informational picture books are forgiving in approach; they are written by authors who recognize that student readers are probably new to their subject and so limit their technical terminology.

They also provide enough information to adequately discuss new concepts. Vague, cursory, clipped, and generalized language, such as that typically found in student textbooks (see the following example), is avoided. Here the authors are describing the Declaration of Independence:

> In the first section, he [Thomas Jefferson] stated a bold idea that each citizen has natural rights that government cannot give or take away. These included rights to 'life, liberty, and the pursuit of happiness.' The purpose of the government was to make sure that all people could enjoy these rights. (Armento et al. 1994, 265)

Is this supposed to make sense to a middle-school child? (Or anyone else?) What is meant by "natural rights"? What does "life, liberty, and the pursuit of happiness" mean to a child? Where are the vivid examples, the specifics that would make sense out of this language?

Picture books take students deeper into highly specialized territory often given rudimentary treatment by conventional social studies or science textbooks. They can provide detailed, behind-the-scenes background information that more traditional texts cannot because they must cover broad time spans in limited amounts of space. How fortunate are the students who read Robert Burleigh's (1991) picture book *Flight* as opposed to those who more typically just read about Charles Lindbergh in an encyclopedia.

> A telephone wire stretches across the far end of the field. To touch this wire will plunge the plane to the ground. There is an extra fuel tank in front of the cockpit. Because of this, Lindbergh cannot see straight ahead. Will the *Spirit of St. Louis*, with its over 5,000 pounds, rise into the air? To keep the plane lighter, Lindbergh is leaving behind his radio and parachute. Will that be enough? He has been up all night getting ready. A thought runs back and forth through his mind: It is still possible to turn back. To return home. (Burleigh 1991, 5)

Somehow, after reading this, I don't think that I, even as an adult, will ever forget that Lindbergh left his parachute behind and that he was downright scared. In making him more human, he was made more memorable in my eyes. I can also clearly envision the fuel tank in front of the cockpit and Lindbergh trying to peer around from its side. This is what learning should be all about—assisting students in creating memorable images.

Farris and Fuhler (1994) offer several good picture books for use in the following subject areas: anthropology, geography, history, and sociology, and (as this sophisticated subject list would lead one to believe) make the point that picture books are no longer just for lower-elementary–aged students, but can be used productively throughout junior and senior high school. In addition, because most picture books are short, several can be read in a relatively short time; with each book read on the same or similar topic but approached from a different context, concepts become more firmly entrenched.

Teachers have reported much success with using picture books to model mathematical concepts by example. In *Fact and Fiction: Literature Across the Curriculum*, Cohn and Wendt (1993) describe how Bonnie Glass, a first-grade teacher, used the big-book version of *The Doorbell Rang* by Pat Hutchins (1970) to teach rudimentary division. As she read the story aloud, her assistant and students acted out each part of the following scenario at a flannelboard:

> The story begins with mother handing her two children, Sam and Victoria, a plate of twelve chocolate-chip cookies she has just baked. They are pleased to determine that when they divide the delicious cookies, they will each get six. But then the doorbell rings and two more children come in. Sam and Victoria now have to share their twelve cookies with Tom and Hannah, and each child will receive three instead of six. The doorbell keeps ringing and each time more friends arrive Sam and Victoria lose out on more cookies. Finally, Grandma arrives with a new batch of cookies. (Cohn and Wendt 1993, 59)

Picture books provide the means through which personal involvement and affect can take hold of new learnings and make them stick. Those students in Ms. Glass' class, who will subsequently learn more formal ways of doing division, will not forget the "feeling" of division that Sam and Victoria had when they had to divvy up their treasured cookies. Appendix F lists annotated resources for locating children's informational picture books.

Try Readers Theatre

My first introduction to Readers Theatre was through Richard Chenault, an interpreter with an avid interest in the theater. Working together one semester in a reading course, he suggested that we give it a try and he very graciously offered to create a script out of the first chapter of one of the novels assigned to my students. Because first chapters in novels are typically difficult for my students, with characters being encountered for the first time along with an abundance of opening description, I seized the opportunity to try this intriguing approach.

Readers Theatre presents literature to an audience in a way that makes the literature come alive. Texts (primarily fiction), plays, and poems, but certainly not only these genres, are selected for their power—their ability to leave audiences somehow touched by what they have experienced. They are interpreted into scripts with narration that "speaks directly to the audience and establishes the basic situation or theme and links the various segments together" (Coger and White 1982, 30). Characters who stay quietly in our minds during silent reading come to life when students take on their roles and interpret their essence by careful selection of lines.

I was sold on Readers Theatre the moment I saw my students "reading" their lines. Some students read and signed the script at the same time, others read ahead and then interpreted their lines into ASL. Although music stands could have been used, most students held the script in one hand and signed with the other. Richard typed a script that eliminated some background description in order to highlight the conflict among the characters in the opening pages, and included dialogue that reflected the personality traits of each character. Upon completion of the reading, my students understood the characters and conflict set up in the first chapter and were ready to read it in its entirety for homework. In first seeing the chapter in theater form, they were more fluent readers of the full text for a variety of reasons: They now clearly understood who was talking to whom; new vocabulary encountered in the "performance" was remembered for the second reading, and between-the-lines information or information implied but unstated came through in the dramatic way the students, acting as characters, expressed their lines.

Young and Vardell (1993) have suggested that Readers Theatre be woven into works of nonfiction as well.

> By combining Readers Theatre with nonfiction trade books in the content areas, teachers can incorporate content reading and learning with the dynamic and interactive processes of Readers Theatre. Students can retain more information, find greater enjoyment in reading content, and be more actively involved in their learning than in a textbook-based curriculum. (398)

They suggest using informational books with dialogue, offer titles that lend themselves well to being scripted, show sample texts and scripts side by side, and reiterate that it is not necessary to use an entire text—excerpts can be selected. Their article lists detailed guidelines on how to prepare a script and the proviso that students will get more benefit from the experience if they themselves, after having the process modeled, create their own scripts. I don't think this can be emphasized enough. By creating their own scripts, students work closely with text and manipulate it in ways that prove that it is thoroughly understood. By reading, rereading, performing their scripts, and watching the scripts of other students being performed, students can't help becoming better readers and more knowledgeable about the topic of their scripts. A suggested excerpt from *The Puppy Book* by Camilla Jessel (1991) that lends itself well to scripting is offered as follows.

TEXT

Saffy the Labrador is about to have puppies. Since she was mated two months ago with a handsome Labrador called Bobby, her stomach has been slowly swelling. Now in the last week she is so fat she can hardly waddle. She lies down to rest for most of the day and finds it an effort to heave herself up again.

Andrew has been watching her progress carefully. Now he can feel small, jerky movements as the tiny unborn puppies move around inside their mother's womb. "Hey, that one actually jabbed me—they must be really strong!"

Saffy searches for the perfect place to have her puppies. The wolves, her ancestors, had their cubs in the forests, and some ancient instinct makes Saffy want to dig a hollow in the earth for her puppies. She chooses the prettiest flowerbed in the garden. But it's the wrong kind of bed.

At last Saffy's birthing box is ready. Lynn lines it with newspapers, which will make a good, warm surface for the puppies, but can be thrown out when they're dirty.

A few days later, Saffy makes for the birthing box. She is obviously feeling strange. She sits there shivering and starts to puff and pant. The children want to know what's happening. "Saffy is going into labor at last," explains their father. "Until the puppies are fully developed, they are held safely in their mother's womb. But when the nine weeks of pregnancy are completed, the puppies have grown strong enough to be born. Saffy's puffing and shivering are the outward signs that her muscles are slowly flexing—ready to ease the puppies out into the world. Try not to be impatient; her labor will probably last a long time."

SCRIPT

Narrator 1: Saffy the Labrador is about to have puppies. Since she was mated two months ago with a handsome Labrador called Bobby, her stomach has been slowly swelling.

Narrator 2: Now in the last week she is so fat she can hardly waddle. She lies down to rest for most of the day and finds it an effort to heave herself up again.

Andrew:	I've been watching her progress carefully and now I can feel small, jerky movements as the tiny unborn puppies move around inside. Hey, that one actually jabbed me—they must be really strong!
Narrator 1:	Saffy searches for the perfect place to have her puppies.
Narrator 2:	The wolves, her ancestors, had their cubs in the forests, and some ancient instinct makes Saffy want to dig a hollow in the earth for her puppies.
Lynn:	Saffy! You chose the prettiest flowerbed in the garden. That's the wrong kind of bed! Your bed is a special birthing box. I'll line it with newspapers, which will make a good, warm surface for the puppies but can be thrown out when they get dirty.
Narrator 1:	A few days later Saffy makes for the birthing box.
Narrator 2:	She is obviously feeling strange. She sits there shivering and shaking.
Children:	What's happening?
Father:	Saffy is going into labor.
Children:	What does that mean?
Father:	Until puppies are fully developed, they are held safely in their mother's womb. But when the nine months of pregnancy are completed, the puppies have grown strong enough to be born.
Mother:	Saffy's puffing and shivering are the outward signs that her muscles are slowly flexing—ready to ease the puppies into the world. Try not to be impatient; labor will probably last a long time.

The beauty of Readers Theatre is its flexibility. Script writers have the freedom to be as creative as they want. As seen in this example, I changed text into dialogue, added some additional dialogue, used two narrators, and added Lynn and Mother to the cast of characters. The interaction of characters displays the text more visually, more enjoyably, and, ultimately, more memorably. When students read *The Puppy Book* and then are walked through the steps of script creation, they will be able to create scripts themselves and reap additional reading comprehension benefits from the in-depth analysis of text that effective script-creating necessitates.

Create Writing Assignments Requiring Language Choices

Weave new information into different genre forms. Consider how writing can be a tool for learning and how it cannot.

> The premise that writing can be a tool for learning depends on sev-eral concepts, one of which is this very broad understanding of writing: that it occurs any time one's mind is engaged in choosing words to be put on paper. It includes note-taking, list-making, writ-ing down observations and expressing feelings, as well as more tra-ditional activities like writing lab reports, essay test answers, essays or stories. Central to this understanding is the notion of language choice. . . . Writing that involves minimal language choices, such as filling-in-blanks exercises or answering questions with someone else's language—the textbook's or the teacher's—are of limited value in promoting either writing or learning. (Mayher, Lester, and Pradl 1983, 78)

When language choice is the students', they grapple to find appropriate phrases and vocabulary, and the learning takes place in the grappling. It is through grappling that students find new ways to express new understandings; in so doing, these new ways of expres-sion come to be housed and eventually used naturally and perma-nently. In a sense, we could say that one of the primary purposes of an education is to learn new ways of expression; after all; "without finding appropriate technical terms, one cannot explain. . .why Jackson vetoed the Second National Bank Bill or describe how plants get food. . . ." (Mayher, Lester, and Pradl 1983, 79). Being able to explain ideas comprehensively, coherently, and accurately is the signpost of an educated person.

We would not, however, expect inexperienced readers and writ-ers to grapple with, explain, or report new knowledge in formal ways using technical terms. We should, however, expect them (with modelling and assistance) to explain their new learnings in genres that are appealing to them and with which they have some famil-iarity. In *Coming to Know: Writing to Learn in the Intermediate Grades*, Nancie Atwell (1990) lists a host of genres for reporting information. Those with much promise for new readers and writers might be how-to books, where specialized knowledge culled from a unit is shared; picture books, either fictional or informational; oral histories and interviews with older students or adults, supplement-ed with background information and drawings; plays and skits that are written out and then videotaped; friendly letters written to people outside the school in which new learning is described; hypothetical journals or diaries of major figures studied; and conversations between people studied or read about, such as Pocahontas and Captain John Smith.

What worked particularly well in one new-readers-and-writers class of Deaf sixth-graders was a fictionalized story composed after a few weeks of notetaking and reading about life during Roman times. As a beginning book, we used Chisholm's *Living in Roman Times: An Usborne First History* (1992), whose myriad pictures closely reflected captioned text. Captions were interpreted as students watched both pictures and text displayed on an overhead projector. In the first section of the book, readers are introduced to Julius and his family members, and then are taken through a typical day in their lives from the perspective of Julius, the younger of two sons. After notetaking was modelled, the students took notes on their own, recording only what they remembered "reading"—without the book in front of them—on one side of an index card and then their responses to what they learned on the other side.

After reading, taking notes, and discussing responses to what was learned, the teacher of the class, Lillian, and I created our own fictional stories that involved one or more of the characters we had encountered in our study and a fictional conflict situation. I wrote about the dismay of Julius' older sister, Julia, who was not allowed to go to school simply because she was female, and a plan she asked her father to fulfill so that young Roman women would not have to stay home and be tutored. Lillian wrote about the mischief Julius got himself into by hanging around the marketplace after school. These stories were interpreted for the students as they followed the text displayed on an overhead projector to ensure that the intent of our stories was conveyed. We pointed out how we wove facts that we had learned about Roman life into our stories. At this point, I handed out a list of all the characters we had met in our reading, as well as several hypothetical conflict situations based on what we had learned from our study of Roman life. Here is one example:

Julia's mother and father have picked Lucias to be Julia's husband and they have prepared a huge wedding feast. The guests are due to arrive at any moment. Julia refuses to participate. She has decided that only she should decide who she will marry. What does Julia look like as a bride? What is offered at the wedding feast? What is Julia thinking right before the wedding and how does she explain her feelings to her parents? How do her parents react? What eventually becomes of Julia?

Because the students had experience with story-writing, the idea that they were to write a story using some of the information they had learned about Roman times was not a problem. They were given the option of creating any story of their own choosing or to use one of my suggested topics. We made it clear that the questions in the hypothetical situation were not to be "answered," but were to be thought of as questions they might want to refer back to their books to flesh out their stories with appropriate historical facts. Before writing, each topic was thoroughly discussed; during writing, Lillian and I conferenced individually with students either to spur them on with their good work or to offer suggestions. Spelling assistance was given upon request to keep the students moving along with their composing. Once first drafts were completed, students responded to them, as described in Chapter 4, pp. 104–105.

Lillian and I felt that this kind of assignment was a good writing-to-learn assignment:

1. It required imaginative thinking.
2. It built on the knowledge and experiences the students already had.
3. It provided an accessible and enjoyable way of synthesizing old and new knowledge.
4. It provided a natural audience for the written work, which includes but isn't limited to the teacher. (Mayher, Lester, and Pradl 1983, 92)

These characteristics make sense. Any time students are asked to imagine, they will remember the products of their imagination because they created them. Any time students are engaged in and enjoying an assignment, that assignment will more likely be remembered than one that instills little fun. Any time students have a chance to share something with an audience, what they share and the more they share it, the better it will be retained. As this example and the ones that follow intend to show, writing about what one is learning is crucial to learning it. Each time we struggle to put words into meaningful text, we are learning both the content and the form of that text; each time we express our new understandings in different forms or genres, we remember our new learnings even better.

Focus on biography. What does it take to really know a person? Hickerson (1991) claims that "knowing, in the sense of developing familiarity and building a lasting relationship, requires frequent and meaningful encounters in significant settings" (p. 25). When we know people, we know a whole constellation of their traits, many of their experiences, their joys, their sorrows, family tales, their fears, and their aspirations. Such information is so natural and engaging for us to come to know that it can hardly be considered learning. Why is this?

We all want to know how we are doing in life. We like to size ourselves up to get some reading on how we're fitting in, to see how our feelings and experiences are similar to or different from others, to learn how different people handle situations that we either have already encountered or might soon encounter. It is a way of trying out "what might happen" by coming to know what has already happened to others.

There can be no better way to get to know people no longer alive or alive, but inaccessible to us, than to read about their lives. Biography is a perfect genre for inexperienced readers and writers to further reading, writing, and learning across subject areas because it is a form of story and, as such, takes us into the lives of others in ways that hook readers into finding out what happens next. Many of the techniques used to write good stories—character description, scene-setting, lots of real-life detail—are tools of a biographer's trade as well. In addition,

> the subjects of biographies, achievers of note, feed children's interest in understanding what is truly possible. . . .If it is possible for the people described in biographies to overcome obstacles such as ignorance, poverty, misery, fear, and hate, then it must also be possible for the rest of us. This is the very optimistic message that children find in biographies.(Egan 1986, as cited in Zarnowski 1990, 8)

Biographies of today are much better written and more realistic than those written thirty to forty years ago. Skilled authors and illustrators have taken an interest in the genre and now many biographies meet the same standards expected of good nonfiction writing. Wit and humor, informative graphics, and a wider choice of subjects (including contemporary issues) can be found (Wilton 1993). Because people do not live their lives in a vacuum, information about the times and cultures of the people are woven into their biographies. This makes it almost impossible to read biography without learning about the historical, social, and political happenings of the times. Reading books about people involved in science serves as a wonderful introduction to technical fields because the learning of new scientific terms is made more palatable when described as discoveries made or paths taken by real people.

In *Learning About Biographies: A Reading and Writing Approach for Children*, Myra Zarnowski (1990) clearly describes how to teach children to read and write biography. Her suggestions are particularly appropriate for students new to reading and writing and have been put to good use in a fifth-grade class of Deaf students where the life of Abraham Lincoln was studied. Abiding by Zarnowski's criteria for selecting a subject for a biography, the teacher of the class and I felt that Lincoln's life was interesting enough to engage the students and that a study of his life would enable the students to confront several important events in history. Most important, there was enough literature available about Lincoln to sustain an in-depth study.

Because the students in the class were beginning readers and writers and new to the idea of reading and writing biography, we decided to use a combination of easy-to-understand books and picture books that offered detail without being too factual or too overwhelming. We wanted to impart the story of Lincoln's life as opposed to a compilation of facts about who he was and what he accomplished. So that the students could get a solid flavor of Lincoln's younger years, we chose *Abraham Lincoln, The Great Emancipator,* a chapter book by Augusta Stevenson (1959). This book uses conversation judiciously throughout and creates little stories, presented as individual chapters, out of the more telling events in Lincoln's early life. One of the other better books that we used was Jean Fritz's (1993) *Just a Few Words, Mr. Lincoln,* which explains the story behind the Gettysburg Address—again, not just what it was, but the reason for it, how it was written, what was going on in Lincoln's life during the writing of it, and how it was received—in clearly written prose with beautifully illustrated corresponding pictures. Some books that we had thought might be good turned out to jump too quickly from event to event without enough information for the students to sink their teeth into. Although they were written simply and clearly pictured, the books were nothing more than compilations of facts. They needed to have some feelings and experiences that children could identify with breathed into them to be understandable to any young student— Deaf or hearing.

Because the students in the class could not read the books on their own, the books were read aloud by a teacher's assistant while I interpreted them into ASL. The interpretation capitalized on stepping into the role of each character who spoke and using accompanying pictures to point out the meaning of the text as much as possible. After twenty to thirty minutes of reading aloud, students were given time to respond to what they had seen. As the students told what they remembered, we wrote what they said on the board in English. We then asked the students their opinion about what they had contributed in an attempt to have their own interpretation part of their response as much as possible. These opinions were also written on the board. After four or five class periods of reading aloud and modelling notetaking, they started to write their own responses. They could work with a partner or alone, and spelling assistance was given upon request.

When we felt that the students had come to better know Abe Lincoln, we asked them to read over their notes, which were on index cards, and to list the important events in his life. This list was written on the board and students selected one event—a snapshot or one part of Lincoln's life—they wanted to draw and write about in more detail.

> A snapshot consists of a picture of an event and a written description. First, the children are asked to visualize the event, to close their eyes and picture it, and then to draw it. . . . After drawing, the children write about their pictures, telling what is happening. (Zarnowski 1990, 38).

At this point, students were worked with in groups of two. They read their index cards, which contained the information they had selected to report, and discussed it thoroughly with their peer and teacher or teacher assistant. After points were clarified and questions about meaning resolved, the students prepared a rough draft of their event, returning to their index cards only to refresh their memories or check spelling.

When all students had a rough draft of their snapshot, they participated in a writing-response group, sharing the draft with their peers who, with the assistance of a teacher, responded to it by raising questions when meaning was not apparent or by suggesting that certain information be added, deleted, or rearranged. Here is Antonio's second draft of his snapshot.

LINCOLN IS ASSASSINATED

> Abe and Mary going theater. Abe and Mary enjoy watch show. Abe and Mary are sit. Abe had guard. Abe and Mary like show. But guard ignore Abe and back John will kill Abe. John shot Lincoln behind left ear. John like slavery. John must be crazy man. Man five worry Abe die. Abe is die. Mary cried. Miss Abe. Then John police look. John captured. Cop kill John die too.

When snapshots are completed, they are arranged in chronological order going clockwise and pasted on a piece of large oaktag. Jointly, the group then prepares a summary statement that ties together the different snapshots with general comments about the subject's life (Zarnowski 1990).

Zarnowski's snapshot approach provides new readers and writers with the support they need to use reading and writing to learn subject-specific information. Through group interaction, teacher modelling, and reading and writing tasks reasonable for (as of yet) unpracticed readers and writers, the snapshot approach teaches students the basics of research, which they will be able to attack more independently once reading and writing abilities mature. Zarnowski concludes with several fine examples of how the snapshot approach can be extended to include the writing of autobiography and biographies of living subjects available for interview.

Establish Research Apprenticeships. As a parent of a young hearing child just becoming comfortable with reading and writing, I am livid at the nature of some of the assignments she brings home from school—particularly the assignments that require her to do research and write up her findings in a report—given to her as early as the second grade. The esteemed research paper—another subject-specific reading and writing assignment—has good intentions but, unfortunately, falls short of meeting its goal. The crux of the problem is that students—again both Deaf and hearing—most often struggle by themselves, to understand new and difficult text about topics of limited familiarity. This recipe for disaster results in language in final papers that student writers don't themselves understand but hope their teachers will. The language, of course, belongs to the authors of the texts read rather than to the student writers of the texts written. It is unconscionable, then, to ask students who lack extensive reading and writing experience to do research and report findings on their own.

Howard Gardner's (1991) notion of apprenticeships, however, is particularly fitting here:

> An active and sustained participation in an apprenticeship, however, offers a far greater opportunity for understanding. In such long-term relationships, novices have the opportunity to witness on a daily basis the reasons for various skills. . . .They observe competent adults moving readily and naturally from one. . .way of representing knowledge to another. They experience firsthand the consequences of a misguided or misconceived analysis. . . .They undergo a transition from a situation in which much of what they do is based on adult models to one in which they are trying out their own approaches, perhaps with some support or criticism from the master. They can discuss alternatives with more accomplished peers, just as they can provide assistance to peers who have recently joined the team. All these options, it seems to me, guide the student toward that state of enablement—exhibiting the capacity to use skills and concepts in an appropriate way—that is the hallmark of an emerging understanding. (203)

Guiding students toward states of enablement is Gardner's way of saying that students need assistance and support—the more well-known term is "scaffolding"—if they are to learn effectively. With respect to the teaching of reading and writing across the subject areas, teachers need to establish apprentice-like relationships with students where reading and reporting information are modelled and then practiced under a teacher's or more skilled student's guidance—much the way Chapters 3 and 4 speak to the teaching of reading and writing in general. Without such guidance, research assignments for students just coming to terms with reading and writing will be done by parents or copied from the World Book Encyclopedia.

As students become more comfortable with reading and writing and as they continue to practice taking notes from read alouds, they should begin to take notes from their own reading if several prerequisites are first fulfilled. Neophtye researchers need to start doing research about topics that they either know something about or have a strong interest in, for as Donald Graves (1989) says:

> . . . it is much easier to help children learn the process of reporting if they already have some conceptual understanding of the material they will study further. Combining the process of gathering material, abstracting it in notes, organizing the information, and finally writing the report in a voice that sounds like the writer is too tall an order when the concepts contained in the new study are themselves as new as the process. (81)

How much more easy a time my daughter would have had if that second-grade report she was required to do had been on "dogs" or "monkeys" (she wanted a monkey as a pet when she was seven years old)—topics with built-in research questions of a personal nature: Which dogs make the best pets? Can monkeys be kept as pets? What do they eat and how are they cared for?—instead of her required report about New York University assigned to complete the unit her class was studying on "The Community." She barely understood the concept of college. A self-selected topic for research reporting will engender a better final product just as it does for narrative writing if a student's heart is in it. Knowing a student's particular area of expertise or fascination will help teachers guide students in selecting juicy topics and research questions for inquiry.

Easy-to-read informational picture books are a must for research reporting. However, as well-pictured as these books are and as clearly as they may be written, students still need guidance in understanding how to take notes from them. Because the best notes are those that are taken about information that is thoroughly understood, the toughest job for teachers is to ensure that what is read is understood. Teachers must decide if their students' reading abilities are such that they can work independently with assistance or if they need to be guided through the reading. If the latter is the case, students need to initially work together on one topic and teachers need to simultaneously interpret text as students read along (see "Text Interpretation" in Chapter 3). After each section of a particular text is interpreted, teachers should discuss its major points with the class. Students should then write these points, as well as a response to them in their own words, depending more on the discussion than the actual text to formulate their notes. This procedure provides teachers with the opportunity to model ways of abstracting or shortening information. For those students who are readers, circulating among them to discuss what was read before they write notes is crucial. This ensures that what the students write will have been recast and grappled with, further assisting the internalization of new ideas as expressed in new language. In both instances, it is during the discussion that decisions as to what information answers a research question or is pertinent to a research topic make sense to take place.

After information has been gathered, there are myriad ways of organizing it. Teachers of younger students might only want their students to compile the information in the form of an acrostic poem, where the first letter of the subject researched is the beginning letter of a line of information about that subject. Pictures drawn and captioned by students depicting various aspects of the subject researched (similar to the snapshot approach described previously) is another simple way of presenting information. For older students, teachers need to model the best way to order the information gathered in report form so that a reader can understand the subject as clearly as possible. They should explain how one topic might naturally lead to the next. At this time, a peer-to-peer "talk through" of the report might be helpful before students begin to compose a first draft so that the "voice" and authority they use in talking about it can appear in their writing about it.

First drafts should be presented to response groups where suggestions for clarification can be made. Second-draft editing will depend on the purpose of the report (where it is headed), the familiarity of the student with the response-revision process, and the needs of the particular piece in light of the written English abilities of the writer as explained in Chapter 4 (Beginnings of Response and Revision, and Later Response and Revision). Keep in mind that final reports of sixth-graders, for example, could make valuable contributions to the classroom libraries of third- or fourth-graders.

Learning how to write a report takes time. During our school careers, most of us began to write reports in the fifth or sixth grade and sometimes much later. When we did, we suddenly "jumped from the bridge" producing a required ten- to twelve-page report with three references. We didn't choose the subject and we had no notion of how to use our time. Seldom were we actually shown how to choose a subject or take notes by a teacher who actually did the report with us. (Graves 1989, 103)

There probably is no more important tool for learning than knowing how to gather and write up research. But most important things and things good for us do not come easily. It is something that students will get better at over time, each time they create a finished product. And when they do, they will be smarter, more competent readers and writers who will be able to learn more, more easily.

A Sample Theme-based Approach

A simple definition of a theme is that it's a "central idea" (Haggitt 1975, as cited in Walmsley 1994) and an organizing framework for teaching and learning. A theme is something substantive and worth exploring; it provides teachers and students with a focus for their teaching and learning. . .[and] is composed of appropriate activities that explore topics that make up, relate to or stem from the central idea. (Walmsley 1994, p. 3)

In theme teaching, teachers and students learn about a topic in-depth in a variety of ways but primarily through reading, writing, and "talking." They are read to through read-alouds or read together with a teacher through guided and independent reading. They write about what they have learned, do related art activities, and share their new learning or projects via oral presentations. As such, theme teaching lends itself beautifully to integration of the language arts and thereby to a more promising way of getting new information internalized and more thoroughly understood. Theme teaching is typically intense, offering students extended time to read, write, and talk about a topic of interest within a particular theme.

In *Children Exploring Their World: Theme Teaching in Elementary School*, Walmsley (1994) delves into the theory and practice of teaching through themes in Part I, and into specific themes taught by teachers in grades one through six in Part II. What rings true in both the theory and practice sections is recognition that teachers are no longer recipients of curricula, executing someone else's curriculum, but are now the creators of it. Theme teachers are more like college professors who must acquire a certain expertise in a particular domain before and during the teaching of it. They must explore the dimensions of their theme, "bump up" (p. 24) their knowledge about it through extensive reading and discussion with those more knowledgeable, assemble materials, and organize day-to-day activities that will be part and parcel of teaching the theme. A lot of work to be sure, but for teachers to teach so that students may learn, they must provide students with a host of reading, writing and talking opportunities that overlap, thereby extending and enhancing students' subject-area understandings. Joanne Paulson (1994) claims that "students can't become more knowledgeable unless they read widely, read deeply, and enjoy their reading; unless they write widely and enjoy their writing; and unless they engage in a variety of language activities (e.g., performing and sharing)" (218).

At the Maryland School for the Deaf, teacher Nancy Swaiko shared her *Colonial America* theme for her class of eleven- through thirteen-year-olds with me. Her seven students were all profoundly Deaf. Two had Deaf parents, four had signing hearing parents, and one had parents who did not sign. The majority of students were readers who, according to Nancy, enjoyed reading and comfortably read books categorized at about the fifth-grade level.

Nancy's key objective in teaching this unit was to offer her students an overview of life during colonial times, with special emphasis on colonial schooling. The theme was to serve as background preparation for an upcoming class trip to Williamsburg, Virginia. To organize her thinking, she read widely on the topic and devised a chart that outlined the major ideas she wanted to address. She then located literature that incorporated these ideas and meshed with students' abilities and interests. One of her goals was to create a large pool of reading material from which she could both assign texts and offer students choices for their own self-selection of texts. She used her own public library, as well as several anthologies of literature she had access to at her school, to choose a collection of short stories, plays, mini-novels, novels, poetry, and expository prose. Once her collection was assembled, she read through it and categorized it into readings that could be done aloud, independently, and with assistance.

She started her theme with an introductory read-aloud—*Meet Felicity* (Tripp 1991a), which immediately hooked her students because the main character, Felicity, grew up in Williamsburg. For this, as Nancy read the text, she Sign-interpreted what she was reading, stopping every so often to explain, summarize, and let the students in on what images the text was creating in her own mind. After each chapter, students wrote either a letter to Felicity in their journals expressing their opinions, feelings, advice, predictions, wishes, and questions, or a general response to the events of the chapter (see p. 77 for a sample entry). Nancy also kept a response journal that she shared with her students to show them that she valued what she was requesting her students to do enough to do it herself, as well as to model for them the kinds of response that could be included in a journal.

Nancy then guided the students through the beginning chapters of an expository text, *If You Lived in Colonial Times* (McGovern 1964). Through the use of an overhead projector, she slowly signed the students through the very difficult, very descriptive beginnings of the books, paragraph by paragraph. If questions came to mind as she was guiding the reading, she expressed them outright so students could see how active her mind was during reading. If the reading reminded her of some experience or brought another idea to mind, the students "heard" about it as well. In this way, they were given glimpses of the way competent readers interact with text. Students brought these books home to reread on their own.

Simultaneously with the read-alouds and guided reading, either at a different time during the same day or on a different day, students were independently reading their assigned individual books, plays, or short stories. These readings included *The Secret Soldier: The Story of Deborah Sampson* (McGovern 1975), *April Drummer* (Edwards 1981), *The Trial of Peter Zenger* (Nolan 1973), and *Felicity Learns a Lesson* (Tripp 1991b). These readings were "pair/shared," which means that students were assigned books (according to reading abilities and interests) and partners and, after fifteen minutes of independent reading, would share what they had read in their own books with their partner. At this time, students who were having difficulty with their individual readings and were not ready to share with a peer received assistance from Nancy. Upon completion, students added these readings to their reading logs and wrote a response paper specifying for a classsmate why a particular reading was a good selection or why it was not. There were several short stories that Nancy required all students to read on their own, as well as extra-credit reading, mostly from the Felicity series, that (not surprisingly) all students accomplished; they enjoyed *Meet Felicity* and wanted to continue their connection with her.

As their understandings of colonial life were formulating, Nancy introduced both class and individual writing projects that focused on colonial schooling. After seeing a movie about colonial education that provided some background understanding, the students chose subtopics related to schooling (e.g., education laws, education of young women) that they wanted to pursue and formulated questions for which answers would be researched, written up, and presented as part of a short class video documentary. Nancy provided the resources—short articles—and modelled how to paraphrase excerpts from them. When enough information had been gathered, she modelled the procedure for completing a first draft. Students' drafts were then revised in peer-response groups. Revised pieces were practiced and then presented "orally." When it was time to be videotaped, some students' signing closely approximated English; other students first came to know their pieces thoroughly and then interpreted them into ASL. The video was recorded in what is referred to as "The Barracks"—a school building dating back to colonial times, fortunately situated right on the campus of MSD.

In addition to individual segments on colonial schooling, as a class (as Part II of the video), the students wrote a short skit depicting the relationship colonial teachers had with their students. Infused into this skit was information about schooling that the students had gleaned from their research. Both Nancy and her students consider the script to be the most valuable part of their unit. It pulled together much of what the students had learned, but perhaps more important, because they had the autonomy to shape the script in any way they chose, the task instilled in them a sense of ownership and, therefore, the drive for a decent product. Without prodding, students pooled their individual understandings to create (through writing) scenes, characters, dialogue, and stage directions. When loopholes and the need for elaboration were noted, revision was a collaborative effort, which necessitated rereadings and lots of "talk." Nancy commented that much talk was devoted to comparing colonial education with Twentieth Century education, particularly in reference to the demeanor of students. The use of dunce caps and birch rods was apparently a "hot" conversation item. Other talk centered around the kinds of costumes and props they needed and how they would create them.

There were additional writing projects. Students wrote to administrators in Williamsburg at the inception of the theme to request information about entrance fees, appropriate clothing to bring, and suggested amounts of money for souvenirs. While in Williamsburg, the students were required to write in their journals each night during quiet time, responding to what they had seen and learned during the day. Excerpts from selected journals were published in the MSD publication, *The Maryland Bulletin*, and a Frederick, Maryland, publication, *Kids Byline*, which circulates throughout the United States. Upon return from Williamsburg, students wrote a short story from the point of view of a colonial child. A suggested title for this was "An Adventure in Williamsburg." Students added these stories to their writing portfolios after sharing them with their peers.

For the artistic portion of the theme, students were required to choose any book from the unit they had read and create one of the following products:

- a diorama (shoebox display of any interesting aspect of the book)
- an ABC chart (facts related to colonial living, drawn and arranged alphabetically)
- gameboard that represents Colonial America (where classmates must answer questions related to colonial living to accrue points or move across the board to an end point)

In addition, each student, following written directions, made his or her own horn book and inscribed letters and numbers in it with a quill pen.

In total, theme projects and the trip to Williamsburg lasted approximately three months, with the artistic and videotaping portions spilling over into a fourth.

When Nancy asked her students which part of the theme they found most enjoyable, all reported that when they were provided time to talk as a group about a book—during or after reading aloud or guided reading—seemed to be the times when they learned and enjoyed learning the most. Creating their own gameboards also received rave reviews. When I asked Nancy which part of the theme she felt really worked and which did not, she also saw the tremendous benefit students got from "listening" to each other's responses about what they had read, but expressed frustration over the lack of time she had to respond in writing to each student's reading journal. She had conferenced with each student in Sign but, in retrospect, thought that a personal written response would have been more beneficial for the students because it would have provided increased exposure to English in print.

Nancy Swaiko swears by thematic units. As ways of intensifying exposure to understandings through the various paths of signing, reading, writing, performing, and creating, they make perfect sense. For students who are on the road to becoming more fluent readers and writers, the support garnered from the interplay of the various modes of learning serves to cement new understandings and, in turn, ways of expressing them through signing, reading, and writing.

Assessing What Students Have Learned

Given the foregoing suggested ways of using reading and writing in the subject areas, it might seem contradictory to say that in the end, when teachers and students step back and ask, "What have you/I learned?," it is the understandings accomplished that should be scrutinized more than the achievement in reading and writing. This does not mean that reading and writing competencies should be overlooked. It means that for students who are still at the beginning stages of becoming readers and writers, technical perfection needs to take a backseat to understandings. In other words, students need to be applauded for what they have learned although their understandings are expressed in nonconventional ways. However, teachers and fellow students should not have to struggle to discern a particular student's intent. Clarity of expression should be expected; grammatical perfection should not.

Current thinking regarding how best to evaluate student understandings in the subject areas (Collins 1990; Gardner 1991; Nelson 1994) underscores several key notions. First is the idea that both the learning and the path traversed by students to that learning need to be assessed. This entails evaluation of both product and process. With respect to product, Gardner claims that, "meaningful projects taking place over time and involving various forms of individual and group activity are the most promising vehicles for learning" (p. 204). Such projects recycle concepts set up to be investigated at the beginning of units or themes, and can run the gamut from the kinds of writing projects described previously and in Atwell (1990) to the more artistic expressions as done by students in Nancy Swaiko's class. It helps to show students examples of what final products are expected to look like; through close examination, teachers and students can define criteria that characterize the work seen. This close examination and discussion should transpire at the inception of all projects. Projects should be selected by the students and reflect the following request, as coined by Patricia Collins (1990): [Pick a project that] "tell[s] me what you know about your topic in a way that you find interesting" (p. 31).

Process evaluation should transpire in the context of on-going, daily project activities through teacher observations and anecdotals. Students' notes, drafts, and responses to and from their classmates all serve as fodder for teachers and students to see how work is progressing. By valuing work-in-progress, students get a real sense that the steps to a final product are an integral part of it, and that good work does not happen quickly. Receiving feedback and assistance along the way also makes what appears to be an overwhelming task much less onerous.

Nancy Swaiko learned a lot about her students' reading, writing, and learning by noting changes in their reading journal entries over time. Responses to beginning chapters of *Meet Felicity* were rehashes of what happened in the chapter, but responses to later chapters became more personalized. As students, over time, shared and responded to each other's and Nancy's journal entries and saw the multiple ways of responding to text, and as their understandings of the story became more fully developed, they started to empathize with the character and to offer suggestions from their own experiences for ways out of particular predicaments. They began to question the character's motives and to predict the effects of certain actions.

Teachers should get creative with assessment. They should trust themselves enough to know that only they know what their students were responsible for learning and what their students had adequate opportunities to learn. Because they know their students best, they can design projects of interest for them and describe their progress along the way. If students are made aware of what is required of them, and if they are shown examples and guided along the way in their completion, assessment will become an active, enjoyable, beneficial, and unobtrusive part of their school day. . .far from the dreaded, cram-the-night-before-one-shot test or assigned-out-of-class research paper of little value for students who do not need to tackle a first language, along with learning reading and writing and, therefore, of even much less value for students who do.

Chapter Six

Conclusion

Some Additional Thoughts

During the writing of this book, thoughts would occasionally confront me that were important to be shared yet disruptive in a particular chapter or as a footnote or addendum. When I noticed that I had filled an entire page with such thoughts, it was time to consider a serious home for them; hence so, "Some Additional Thoughts" section.

Evaluating ASL Proficiency

It is unconscionable to think that teachers of Deaf students do not have to demonstrate expressive and receptive competencies in the language they use all day with their students. Although many teachers might be competent in expressing themselves in textbook ASL, their abilities to *communicate* with their students can be a different story. As a two-way process, communication necessitates that teachers and students understand each other, and Deaf students, as inexperienced language users, do not always sign in ways that teachers of Sign Language do. Teachers need to know the meanings their students make in Sign Language, and conversely, need to be able to express themselves in ASL in ways that Deaf students understand—similar to the ways discussed in Chapter 2. Interchanges between teachers and students or snippets of classroom interaction need to be analyzed and used to improve performance. Therefore, tests of Sign Language proficiency that seek an "idealized" proficiency should be set aside for more context-based, holistic evaluations that describe Sign Language performance in classroom contexts with real students.

Adopt a Family

Sign Language classes for parents in schools for Deaf children or learning centers set up exclusively to introduce parents to the language and culture of Deaf people are often dismally attended, but not for parents' lack of interest or desire to help their children. With child care and work responsibilities, parents are busy people. A more personal and time-flexible approach might be tried wherein Deaf families and/or Deaf teens or young adults "adopt" a hearing family in their neighborhood. Deaf parents or teens could read stories to their adopted family members; view tapes on the language and culture of the Deaf community with them; interpret captioned movies and television shows; play computer games, board games, cards; bake; or participate in "pretend" play with younger children. As long as the contexts for interaction are initially kept supportive—as long as members of both families see some of what is being "talked" about—communication will proceed smoothly. High-school Deaf students might fulfill community-service credit by participating in such a program.

Teacher Training Programs

Prospective teachers of Deaf students need to take the same courses that prospective teachers of hearing students take. I do not see a place for distinct "Methods and Materials" courses for teachers of Deaf students if methodologies and materials are essentially the same as those used with hearing children. (This, of course, presupposes that the courses offer facilitative and supportive contexts for learning, as described in Chapter 5.) What is crucial are intensive ASL courses—perhaps fifteen hours per week—in which hearing students learn not only the language, but how to use it to interpret text (see Chapter 3) for the teaching of reading. Models of storytelling, reading aloud, and reading instruction need to be studied in depth, along with tapes that show Deaf children signing in naturalistic settings (e.g., the schoolyard or cafeteria).

In addition, there need to be courses on the linguistics of ASL, ASL and English language development, and Deaf culture. Because we know so little about language development in Deaf students, end-term projects for students need to focus on descriptions of ASL to document the kinds of growth that can be expected. This would require that students learn how to transcribe the Sign Language Deaf children use, which would be immeasurably helpful in learning what hearing teachers find so problematic to understand. Documenting the paths of reading and writing development for selected Deaf students would also make valuable end-term projects.

ASL Arts as Opposed to ASL Classes

If ASL is the language of instruction all day long at schools for Deaf students, I am perplexed at the need to have classes in which ASL is taught. Students will tacitly acquire the rules of ASL ever more productively in natural situations, such as those described throughout this book, than by practicing dialogues and drills from ASL textbooks. More intriguing ways of learning the bountifulness of the language is to study its wordplay, lore, humor, poetry, and dramatic expressiveness. "The possibilities for this new art form in Sign seem bounded only by the imagination within the community itself" (Wolkomir 1992, 40).

Speech Teaching

Just as there are many Deaf people who are able to speak and lipread well, so are there Deaf students with the propensity to also speak and lipread well—typically the post-lingually deafened and those with substantial amounts of residual hearing. These students should receive early auditory stimulation and vocal practice, but, not beyond the linguistic stage that they are at in their acquisition of English. Practicing phrases much beyond the complexity of what is picked up from immersion in natural oral contexts would be more a memorization task than a natural English-language learning task.

Speech teaching might, at some point, closely tie in with students' attempts at becoming better readers and writers. Peter deVilliers (personal communication, December 1993) commented that oral Deaf children tend to master complex English constructions from written English rather than from immersion in natural oral discourse. Speech teachers, then, might want to work with students' pronunciation of their own edited informal letters, journal entries, stories, or scripts. As students progress in their abilities, conversations about familiar topics already read and written about can be tried. Aside from special times for speech and lipreading work, students with substantial amounts of residual hearing should be educated along with their Deaf peers in ASL.

Evolving Meaning-driven and Reciprocal Ways to Educate Deaf Students

It would be dishonest of me to let you believe that I have always practiced what I have "preached" in this book. When I first started out as a teacher, aside from the fact that I was "not allowed" to use

ASL with my students, my teaching was a far cry from being mean-ing-driven and reciprocal. When I taught second- and third-grade children, I thought that what they needed most was vocabulary. I spent nights cutting out pictures of household appliances, animals, furniture, clothing, and food, and days teaching the signs for them along with other assorted memorized greetings, requests, and lan-guage patterns. Additional "language teaching" included inordinate amounts of language-experience work which essentially ended up being inordinate amounts of copying from the blackboard and little more. Because there were very few books to read and little, if any, social studies or science taught (students first had to be immersed in language), there were few ideas to talk about and thereby few understandings students were coming away with. My focus was on language, language, language, but, unfortunately, only for its own cause and not put to use in the service of acquiring understandings. There was, and still is, nothing very interesting about learning how to sign "The book is on the table."

Teaching older students, I started experimenting with using an opaque projector to teach reading. However, still constrained to fol-low Signed English as dictated by school policy, I found myself los-ing my students' interest, most likely because what I was signing was virtually a carbon copy of what the text was and not very help-ful for them as inexperienced English users, and most likely also because my book choice was an adapted one and, more often than not (back then), largely unappealing.

There were logistical problems as well. The air current from the motor of the projector made the pages of the book flap up and down, and I was unable to flatten the book out enough so that text along-side the binding could be seen. We resorted to using copies of books for each student and tapping on desks to get each other's attention when some students were ready to answer questions (I devised) while others were still reading. There was little discussion of thoughts or feelings about what was read, primarily because there was little to think or feel about in our rather mind-numbing reading. If the students understood the text, they displayed good "reading comprehension." But what ideas did they come away with? What did they learn?

My teaching of writing at upper-grade levels was also similarly unremarkable. I was starting to hear about "writing process," but its tenets did not initially assist me in dealing with the kind of writing my students generated. They were writing fluently but hardly clear-ly, and because I did not know how to handle major clarity and cor-rectness concerns, I "just let them write," which was a popular notion at the time. Response and revision were ideas just coming to be known. But what were my students getting out of this? What were they learning? These questions gnawed at me. There was an omnipresent feeling that something was not the way it should be, irrespective of the fact that ASL was still the forbidden language.

It would be unfair to say that nothing changed, pedagogically speaking, during my starting-out years as a public-school teacher, because a lot did change. Consultants from New York University introduced me and my colleagues to the idea of the nonteaching of a first language and the importance of keeping understandings to be conveyed, first and foremost, as our teaching goals and our teaching contexts as facilitative as possible. In no uncertain terms, they showed us how the idea of being language teachers—to the point of almost being language "therapists"—had consumed us and obliterated our primary mission as educators. They introduced us to the concept of theme teaching. For a while, I felt as if I were teaching at an exclusive private school for Deaf students—the barriers to language acquisition, which we had unknowingly created, started tumbling down as students started having something to say. As they learned ideas from their subject-area–based hands-on activities, they evolved the language (a halting, plodding form of English-Sign, but a substantially more robust form of ASL) to show us that, yes, they could learn ideas and acquire language at the same time.

But the reading-writing-learning-connection questions still gnawed at me. I was searching for ways that would allow me to offer my students the kind of reading and writing opportunities that would do more than just enable them to "comprehend" text and write clearly; the kind of activities that would assist my students in finding more than the main idea and supporting details of a passage and more than ways of using writing as a way of practicing control of written English. Just as I had learned not to be a language therapist, it was now time to learn how not to be a reading/writing "specialist." I wanted my students to love reading and writing and to walk away from reading and writing experiences a little more knowledgeable about themselves and the workings of the world. My opportunity to create these ways of teaching came with a job offer from LaGuardia Community College to teach courses in developmental reading and writing for Deaf students who were not yet considered college-level readers and writers.

Having been forbidden to use ASL for some twelve years, you can imagine how stunned I was at my job interview when it was just assumed that my instruction would be all in ASL. I don't think it will be a digression to add that my interviewers were not from the field of Deaf Education. One was a social worker, one an ASL teacher, and the other a counselor. The teacher and counselor were

Deaf. The reason the position I was applying for was created was to stem the tide of failure Deaf students were experiencing in their mainstream reading and writing classes, where they were placed with interpreters and notetakers. My interviewers saw the need for the use of ASL and for a teacher with experience teaching reading and writing to Deaf students. Other than having my teaching supervised and evaluated by the Chairs of the Communication Skills and English departments, I would be free to teach how I saw fit.

But the freedom to use ASL and the autonomy to teach as I wished did not instantaneously transform my teaching practices. I found myself clinging to traditional ways of teaching reading, which were justified by my answer "They can't" to questions I kept hearing in my mind: How could they get meaning from print unless I showed them the signs for all the words? How could inexperienced readers read college-level books? How could they discuss "the important parts" of an assignment unless I brought these topics up for discussion? How could they judge whether they were improving as readers unless I tested them on a "fair" (norm-referenced) test?

It was through observations of my students either in the process of understanding new ideas or experiencing difficulty with certain tasks that led me to rethink these questions and my answers to them. My first observation was that when I used an overhead projector to display text and interpreted the text alongside it (see Chapter 3), my students sat riveted to both the interpretation and the text. Such intense attention I assumed meant that the interpretation was assisting them in making meaning out of print. To test my assumption, I started asking my students to reread interpreted sections silently. Their head-nods, "AH" signs, and deeper understandings as expressed in Sign were indications that connections were being made.

Given my students' reactions to interpreted text, I started thinking that perhaps instead of unduly worrying about readability of text—the complexity of language used—I should shift my emphasis from language to content and select books with meaty, interesting happenings and messages—even for inexperienced readers. With interpretation assistance, students would gradually understand more after they had seen problematic passages interpreted and had a chance to reread them. I also began thinking that my teaching of reading should perhaps be more process-like. Students could try reading and responding to an assignment as best they could on their own, then participate in a discussion of it that would include referring back to the text when problematic parts needed interpretation. Those students who had great difficulty with certain parts would be encouraged to rewrite their written responses after the benefit of interpretation and class discussion. Understandings, then, would be gradually created—starting with a first pass, which was an initial read and written response; then moving toward clearer understandings through discussion, interpretation, rereading; and finally even clearer connections through the act of rewriting.

My second observation was that students had their own important parts to talk or raise questions about from their reading; nine times out of ten, these parts were not necessarily those that I would have pinpointed for class discussion. Typically, they would be portions of text that "hit" students because at the time of the reading, some reflection of themselves or a current personal concern was noted. I also saw that the more students talked, the more students "listened." Because classmates are far more interesting to pay attention to than teachers, from a student's perspective at least, I learned to say less.

Still another observation was that while I knew my students were improving as readers, this growth was not evident on their required departmental exit exam. I came to realize that the exam did not reflect my emerging stance on the nature of reading and reading instruction for inexperienced readers. If learning to read and reading instruction work best within supportive contexts, any test of reading ability must be administered in just those kinds of contexts. If my students were reading about a particular subject area and writing responses to their readings, I gradually came to realize that any test of their abilities as readers should embody both the content and form of the instruction in which they participated.

My "how could" and "they can't" thinking persisted for about a year, but by the start of my second year, I had realigned my methodologies with observations of my students' learning (and nonlearning) that beckoned me to change. I must admit, though, to having had similar kinds of "how-could"-type questions for the teaching of writing as well. Initially, I was wary about inexperienced readers and writers responding to the writing of more accomplished peer-writers. I also had difficulty coming to terms with the teaching of grammar—the how and the when of it—as well as the degree to which essays needed to be edited given the grave inexperience with writing many of my students displayed. But again, it was the day-to-day observations of what was and wasn't working in my own classroom that modified both the theory behind my teaching and its practice. My students showed me that, yes, at times, less-proficient readers and writers did struggle to understand the writing of some classmates, but they could come to understand this writing and eventually become stronger readers and writers by participating in discussions in response groups. They also showed me that teaching the grammar of Wh-question formation, how to use question words such as who, what, where, when, and why as an example, carries over to questions they write as part of their written responses to text, and that "slow reads" of edited pieces assisted them in remembering specific language for use in other written work. My students, more than any textbook on "Deafness," have shown me how they learn best. However, I had to first learn to question the effectiveness of my work, and then seek ways within my own classroom to find answers.

I often wonder how my teaching will change in the next couple of years. Right now I'm thinking about how I might better approach the research paper that I do jointly with my students in my reading class and how I might be able to squeeze more reading into my writing class. Sometimes I think that when I became a teacher I accepted a special mission to work on a huge jigsaw puzzle. Each year the puzzle comes more and more into shape, but only after I spend time replacing pieces that do not fit with ones that do. The key is getting the right fit. It takes a lot of time, thought, and hard work, but as we reflect on our accomplishments, there is a sense of satisfaction in seeing that the work has been purposeful. It is never too late to work on the puzzle because it is never done—it just keeps getting better. As we approach the Twenty-first Century, I invite you to work on this puzzle—to reimagine and reconstruct the best possible ways of educating Deaf students.

References

Abrams, M. 1996. "A Place Where Children Thrive." *Preview* (Spring): 9–12.

Ahlgren, I. 1982. *Sign Language and the Learning of Swedish by Deaf Children.* Stockholm: National Swedish Board of Education.

Anderson, M., N. Boren, J. Caniglia, and E. Krohn. 1980. *Apple Tree.* Beaverton, OR: Dormac, Inc.

Andrews, J., and N. Taylor. 1987. "From Sign to Print: A Case Study of Picture Book Reading Between Mother and Child." *Sign Language Studies* 56 (Fall): 261–274.

Andrews, J., and K. Gonzales. 1992. "Free Writing of Deaf Children in Kindergarten." *Sign Language Studies* 74 (Spring): 63–78.

Applebee, A. N. 1978. *The Child's Concept of Story.* Chicago, IL: The University of Chicago Press.

Armento, B., J. Jorge Klor de Alva, G. Nash, C. Salter, L. Wilson, and K. Wixson. 1994. *America Will Be.* Boston, MA: Houghton Mifflin Company.

"ASL Position Paper Approved by NAD," *The NAD Broadcaster* March, 1994: 39.

Atwell, N. 1990. "Genres for Report Writing." In *Coming to Know: Writing to Know in the Intermediate Grades*, ed. N. Atwell, 163–165. Portsmouth, NH: Heinemann.

Baker, L. 1985. "How Do We Know When We Don't Understand? Standards for Evaluating Text Comprehension." *Metacognition, Cognition, and Human Performance*, eds. D. L. Forrest-Pressley, G. E. MacKinnon, and T. G. Waller, 155–205. Orlando, FL: Academic Press.

Barrs, M., S. Ellis, H. Hester, and A. Thomas. 1988. *The Primary Language Record.* Portsmouth, NH: Heinemann.

Bellugi, U. 1980. "Clues from the Similarities Between Signed and Spoken Language." In *Signed and Spoken Language: Biological Constraints on Linguistic Form*, eds. U. Bellugi and M. Studdert-Kennedy, and Weinheim. Deerfield Beach, FL: Verlag Chemie.

Bernstein, M., M. Maxwell, and K. Matthews. 1985. "Bimodal or Bilingual Communication." *Sign Language Studies* 47 (Summer): 127–140.

Berthoff, A. 1981. *The Making of Meaning.* Montclair, NJ: Boynton/Cook.

Berthoff, A. 1993. "What Works? How Do We Know?" *Journal of Basic Writing* 12 (2): 3–17.

Bissex, G. 1980. *Gnys at Wrk: A Child Learns to Write and Read.* Cambridge, MA: Harvard University Press.

Block, E. 1992. "See How They Read: Comprehension Monitoring of L1 and L2 Readers." *TESOL Quarterly* 28 (2): 319–338.

Bornstein, H., K. Saulnier, and L. Hamilton. 1980. "Signed English: A First Evaluation." *American Annals of the Deaf* 125 (4): 467–481.

Bornstein, H., K. Saulnier, and L. Hamilton. 1981. "A Brief Follow-up to the First Evaluation." *American Annals of the Deaf* 126 (1): 69–72.

Boyle, O., and S. Peregoy. 1990. "Literacy Scaffolds: Strategies for First- and Second-Language Readers and Writers." *The Reading Teacher* 44 (3): 19–200.

Britton, J. 1970. *Language and Learning.* London: Penguin.

Brown, R., and C. Hanlon. 1970. "Derivational Complexity and Order of Acquisition." *In Cognition and the Development of Language*, ed. J. R. Hayes, 11–53. New York: Wiley and Sons, Inc.

Burleigh, R. 1991. *Flight.* New York: Philomel.

Campione, J.C., and A.L. Brown. 1985. *Dynamic Assessment: One Approach and Some Initial Data.* (Technical Report No. 361). Urbana, IL: Center for the Study of Reading.

Carrasquillo, A. 1990. "The Role of Native Language Instruction in Bilingual Education Programs." *Language Association Bulletin 52* (November): 10–12.

Chisholm, J. 1992. *Living in Roman Times: An Usborne First History.* London: Usborne Publishing Ltd.

Chomsky, C. 1980. "Stages in Language Development and Reading Exposure." *In Thought and Language/Language and Thought*, eds. M. Wolf, M. McQuillan, and E. Radwin, 201–229. Cambridge, MA: Harvard Educational Review.

Clay, M. 1972. *The Patterning of Complex Behavior.* London: Heinemann.

Clay, M. 1991. *Becoming Literate: The Construction of Inner Control.* Portsmouth, NH: Heinemann.

Coger, L., and M. White. 1982. *Readers Theatre Handbook.* Glenview, IL: Scott Foresman and Company.

Cohn, D., and S. Wendt. 1993. "Literature Adds up For Math Class." In *Fact and Fiction: Literature Across the Curriculum*, ed. B. Cullinan, 57–67. Newark, DE: International Reading Association.

Cokely, D. 1986. "The Effects of Lag Time on Interpreter Errors." *Sign Language Studies* 53 (Winter): 341–376.

Collins, P. 1990. "Bridging the Gap." In *Coming to Know: Writing in the Intermediate Grades*, ed. N. Atwell, 17–31. Portsmouth, NH: Heinemann.

Crawford, J. 1991. *Bilingual Education: History, Politics, Theory and Practice.* Los Angeles, CA: Bilingual Education Services, Inc.

Cummins, J. 1994. "Knowledge, Power, and Identity in Teaching English as a Second Language." *In Educating Second Language Children: The Whole Child, the Whole Curriculum, the Whole Community,* ed. F. Genesee, 33–58. New York: Cambridge University Press.

Dale, P. 1970. *Language Development: Structure and Function.* New York: Holt, Rinehart and Winston.

Damasio, A., and H. Damasio. 1993. "Brain and Language." In *Mind and Brain: Readings from Scientific American,* 54–65. New York: W.H. Freeman and Company.

Davidson, D. 1980. "Current Approaches to the Teaching of Grammar in ESL." In *Readings on English as a Second Language,* ed. K. Croft, 317–338. Cambridge, MA: Winthrop Publishers, Inc.

Davies, S. 1991. "Bilingual Education of Deaf Children in Sweden and Denmark: Strategies for Transition and Implementation." *Sign Language Studies* 71 (Summer): 169–195.

deVilliers, P. 1993. Letter to author, December.

Dyson, A. 1995. "When Children Write to Persuade: What We Need to Know About Children in the Primary Grades." In *Briefs On Writing* (March): 1–4. (Available from the University of California, National Center for Writing and Literacy, Berkeley)

Edelsky, C. 1986. *Writing in a Bilingual Program: Habia una Vez.* Norwood, NJ: Ablex.

Edelsky, C. B. Altwerger, and B. Flores. 1991. *Whole Language: What's the Difference?* Portsmouth, NH: Heinemann.

Edwards, C. 1981. *April Drummer.* Boston, MA: Houghton Mifflin Company.

Egan, K. 1986. *Teaching as Storytelling: An Alternative Approach to Teaching and Curriculum in the Elementary School.* Chicago: The University of Chicago Press.

Elbow, P. 1981. *Writing with Power.* New York: Oxford University Press.

Ewoldt, C. 1981. "Factors Which Enable Deaf Readers to Get Meaning From Print." In *Learning to Read in Different Languages,* ed. S. Hudelson, 45–53. Washington, DC: Center for Applied Linguistics.

Ewoldt, C. 1985. "A Descriptive Study of the Developing Literacy of Young Hearing-impaired Children." In *Learning to Write and Writing to Learn,* ed. R. Kretschmer, 109–126. Washington, DC: The Alexander Graham Bell Association for the Deaf.

Ewoldt, C. 1990. "The Early Literacy Development of Deaf Children." In *Educational and Developmental Aspects of Deafness,* eds. D. Moores and K. Meadow-Orlans, 85–114. Washington, DC: Gallaudet University Press.

Farris, P., and C. Fuhler. 1994. "Developing Social Studies Concepts Through Picture Books." *The Reading Teacher* 47 (5): 380–387.

Filichia, P. "The King's Interpreters: The Hands Are As Quick As the I." *New Jersey Star-Ledger*. October 1996. 21.

Fitzgerald, E. 1937. *Straight Language for the Deaf*. Washington, DC: The Steck Company.

Fritz, J. 1993. *Just a Few Words, Mr. Lincoln*. New York: Grosset & Dunlop.

Gardner, H. 1991. *The Unschooled Mind: How Children Think and How Schools Should Teach*. New York: HarperCollins Publishers, Inc.

Garvey, C. 1977. *Play*. Cambridge: Harvard University Press.

Gee, J.P., and W. Goodhart. 1988. "ASL and the Biological Capacity for Language." In *Language Learning and Deafness*, ed. M. Strong, 49–74. New York: Cambridge University Press.

Genesee, F. 1994. "Introduction." In *Educating Second Language Children: The Whole Child, the Whole Curriculum, the Whole Community*, ed. F. Genesee, 1–12. New York: Cambridge University Press.

Goswami, U. 1986. "Children's Use of Analogy in Learning to Read: A Developmental Study." *Journal of Experimental Child Psychology* 42 (1): 73–83.

Graves, D. 1983. *Writing: Teachers and Children at Work*. Portsmouth, NH: Heinemann.

Graves, D. 1989. *Investigate Nonfiction*. Portsmouth, NH: Heinemann.

Greenberg, J. 1970. *In This Sign*. New York: Henry Holt.

Haggitt, E.M. 1975. *Projects in the Primary School*. London: Longman.

Hakuta, K. 1986. *Mirror of Language: The Debate on Bilingualism*. New York: Basic Books.

Hancock, M. 1993. "Exploring and Extending Personal Response Through Literature Journals." *The Reading Teacher* 46 (6): 446–474.

Hansen, B. 1980. "Research on Danish Sign Language and Its Impact on the Deaf Community in Denmark." In *Sign Language and the Deaf Community*, eds. C. Baker and R. Battison, 24–263. Silver Spring, MD: National Association of the Deaf.

Harste, J., V. Woodward, and C. Burke. 1984. *Language Stories and Literacy Lessons*. Portsmouth, NH: Heinemann.

Heinig, R. 1992. *Improvisation with Favorite Tales: Integrating Drama into the Reading/Writing Classroom*. Portsmouth, NH: Heinemann.

Helfer, A. 1991. *Scared Stiff and Other Creepy Tales*. Racine, WI: Western Publishing Company.

Hickerson, B. 1991. "Teaching Content Area Vocabulary: The Wrong Way and Several Right Ways." *Reading Today* (August/September): 25.

Hill, E. 1981. *Spot's First Walk*. New York: Penguin Books.

Hudelson, S. 1984. "Kan yu Ret an Rayt en Ingles: Children Become Literate in English as a Second Language." *TESOL Quarterly* 18 (2): 22 1–238.

Hudelson, S. 1994. "Literacy Development of Second Language Children." In *Educating Second Language Children: The Whole Child, the Whole Curriculum, the Whole Community,* ed. F. Genesee, 129–158. New York: Cambridge University Press.

Hutchins, P. 1970. *The Doorbell Rang.* New York: Greenwillow.

IRA/NCTE Joint Task Force on Assessment. 1994. *Standards for the Assessment of Reading and Writing.* The International Reading Association and the National Council of Teachers of English.

Jessel, C. 1991. *The Puppy Book.* Cambridge, MA: Candlewick Press.

Johnson, M. 1987. *The Body in the Mind: The Bodily Basis of Meaning, Imagination and Reason.* Chicago: University of Chicago Press.

Johnson-Laird, P. 1983. *Mental Models: Toward a Cognitive Science of Language, Inference, and Consciousness.* Cambridge, MA: Harvard University Press.

Johnson, R., S. Liddell, and C. Erting. 1989. *Unlocking the Curriculum: Principles for Achieving Access in Deaf Education.* Washington, DC: Gallaudet University.

Kelly, L. 1990. "Cognitive Theory Guiding Research in Literacy and Deafness." In *Educational and Developmental Aspects of Deafness,* eds. D. Moores and K. Meadow-Orlans, 202–231. Washington, DC: Gallaudet University Press.

Kelly, L. 1993. "Recall of English Function Words and Inflections by Skilled and Average Deaf Readers." *American Annals of the Deaf* 138 (3): 288–296.

Kendig, F. 1983. "A Conversation with Roger Schank." *Psychology Today* in (April): 28–34.

Khalsa, D.K. 1987. *I Want a Dog.* New York: Crown Publishers.

Kimmel, M., and E. Segal. 1991. *For Reading Aloud.* New York: Dell Publishing.

Kirby, D., and T. Liner. 1981. *Inside Out.* Portsmouth, NH:Boynton/Cook.

Klima, E., and U. Bellugi. 1979. *The Signs of Language.* Cambridge, MA: Harvard University Press.

Knoblauch, C., and L. Brannon. 1984. *Rhetorical Traditions and the Teaching of Writing.* Portsmouth, NH: Boynton/Cook.

Kobrin, B. 1988. *Eyeopeners! How to Choose and Use Children's Books About Real People, Places and Things.* New York: Penguin Books.

Kuntze, M. 1994. "Developing Students' Literacy Skills in ASL." In *Post Milan ASL & English Literacy: Issues, Trends, & Research,* ed. B. Snider, 267–281. Washington, DC: Gallaudet University, Continuing Education and Outreach.

La Bue, M.A. 1995. "Language and Learning in a Deaf Education Classroom: Practice and Paradox." In *Sociolinguistics in Deaf Communities,* ed. C. Lucas, 164–220. Washington, DC: Gallaudet University Press.

Lakoff, G. 1987. *Women, Fire and Dangerous Things: What Categories Reveal About the Mind.* Chicago: University of Chicago Press.

Lane, H. 1979. *The Wild Boy of Aveyron.* Cambridge, MA: Harvard University Press.

Lartz, M., and L. Lestina. 1995. "Strategies Deaf Mothers Use When Reading to Their Young Deaf or Hard-of-Hearing Children." *American Annals of the Deaf* 140 (4): 358–362.

Limbrick, E.A., S. McNaughton, and M. Clay. 1992. "Time Engaged in Reading: A Critical Factor in Reading Achievement." *American Annals of the Deaf* 137 (4): 309–314.

Livingston, S. 1981. *The Acquisition and Development of Sign Language in Deaf Children of Hearing Parents.* Ph.D. diss., New York University.

Livingston, S. 1983. "Levels of Development in the Language of Deaf Children." *Sign Language Studies* 40 (Fall): 193–286.

Livingston, S. 1986. "An Alternative View of Education for Deaf Children: Part I." *American Annals of the Deaf* 131 (1): 21–25.

Livingston, S., and L. Brannon. 1986. "An Alternative View of Education for Deaf Children: Part II." *American Annals of the Deaf* 131 (3): 229–231.

Livingston, S. 1989. "Revision Strategies of Deaf Student Writers." *American Annals of the Deaf* 134 (1): 21–26.

Livingston, S. 1991. "Comprehension Strategies of Two Deaf Readers." *Sign Language Studies* 71 (Summer): 115–130.

Livingston, S., B. Singer, and T. Abramson. 1993. *The Effectiveness of Two Different Kinds of Interpretation* (Contract No. H133C20084). Washington, DC: National Institute on Disability and Rehabilitation Research.

Livingston, S., B. Singer, and T. Abramson. 1994. "Effectiveness Compared: ASL Interpretation vs. Transliteration." *Sign Language Studies* 82 (Spring): 1–54.

Livingston, S., and M. Collins. 1994. "How to Read Aloud to Deaf Children and Young Adults." In *Post Milan ASL & English Literacy: Issues, Trends & Research,* ed. B. Snider, 63–73. Washington, DC: Gallaudet University, Continuing Education and Outreach.

Lou, M., S. Fischer, and J. Woodward. 1987. "A Language-Independent Measure of Communicative Competence." *Sign Language Studies* 57 (Winter): 353–370.

Lucas, C. 1989. *The Sociolinguistics of the Deaf Community.* New York: Academic Press.

Luetke-Stahlman, B. 1993. "Research-based Language Intervention Strategies Adapted for Deaf and Hard-of-Hearing Children." *American Annals of the Deaf* 138 (5): 404–410.

Lynch, P. 1986. *Using Big Books and Predictable Books.* New York: Scholastic.

Mahshie, S. 1995. *Educating Deaf Children Bilingually.* Washington, DC: Gallaudet University Press.

Mallan, K. 1991. *Children as Storytellers.* Portsmouth, NH: Heinemann.

Marschark, M., R. De Beni, M. Polazzo, and C. Cornoldi. 1993." Deaf and Hard-of-Hearing Adolescents' Memory for Concrete and Abstract Prose." *American Annals of the Deaf* 138 (1): 31–39.

Marshall, H. 1961. "Relations Between Home Experience and Children's Use of Language in Play Interactions with Peers." *Psychological Monographs* 75 (5): 9–15.

Mathabane, M. 1986. *Kaffir Boy.* New York: Penguin Books.

Mather, S. 1990. "Home and Classroom Communication." In *Educational and Developmental Aspects of Deafness,* eds. D. Moores and K. Meadow-Orlans, 232–254. Washington, DC: Gallaudet University Press.

Maxwell, M. 1984. "A Deaf Child's Natural Development of Literacy." *Sign Language Studies* 44 (Fall): 191–224.

Maxwell, M. 1987. "The Acquisition of English Bound Morphemes in Sign Form." *Sign Language Studies* 57 (Winter): 323–352.

Mayher, J., N. Lester, and G. Pradl. 1983. *Writing to Learn/Learning to Write.* Portsmouth, NH: Boynton/Cook.

Mayher, J. 1990. *Uncommon Sense: Theoretical Practice in Language Education.* Portsmouth, NH: Heinemann.

McDonald, M. 1990. *Is This a House for Hermit Crab?* New York: Franklin Watts.

McGovern, A. 1964. *If You Lived in Colonial Times.* New York: Four Winds Press.

McGovern, A. 1975. *The Secret Soldier: The Story of Deborah Sampson.* New York: Scholastic.

McIntire, M. 1992. *The Acquisition of ASL by Deaf Children.* Burtonsville, MD: Sign Media, Inc.

Mellon, J. 1981. "Language Competence." In *The Nature and Measurement of Competency in English,* ed. C. Cooper, 21–64. Urbana, IL: National Council of Teachers of English.

Miller-Nomeland, M., and M. French. 1994. "Developing Stories in ASL and ESL." In *Post Milan ASL & English Literacy: Issues, Trends, & Research,* ed. B. Snider, 253–262. Washington, DC: Gallaudet University, Continuing Education and Outreach.

Moustafa, M. 1993. "Recoding in Whole Language Instruction." *Language Arts* 70 (6): 483–487.

Naidoo, B. 1986. *Journey to Jo'burg.* New York: HarperCollins.

Nelson, C. 1994. "Historical Literacy: A Journey of Discovery." *The Reading Teacher* 47 (7): 552–556.

Nieratka, 1990. Letter to author, 18 April.

Nodset, J. 1988. *Who Took the Farmer's Hat?* New York: HarperCollins.

Nolan, P. 1973. "The Trial of Peter Zenger." In *Patriotic and Historic Plays for Young People,* ed. S. Kamerman, 74–91. Boston, MA: Plays, Inc.

Ohanian, B., and G. Vollmer. 1989. "Word by Word." *Parenting* (October): 65–69.

Otte, G. 1991. "Computer-adjusted Errors and Expectations." *Journal of Basic Writing* 10 (2): 71–86.

Paul, P. 1990. "ASL to English." In *Communication Issues Among Deaf People: A Deaf American Monograph,* ed. M. Garretson, 40 (1,2,3,4): 107–113. Silver Spring, MD: National Association of the Deaf.

Paul, P,. and S. Quigley. 1994. "American Sign Language-English Bilingual Education." In *Language Learning Practices with Deaf Children,* eds. P. McAnally, S. Rose, and S. Quigley, 219–253. Austin, TX: Pro-Ed.

Paulson, J. 1994. "Westward Movement: A Fifth-grade Theme." In *Children Exploring Their World: Theme Teaching in Elementary School,* ed. S. Walmsley, 217–242. Portsmouth, NH: Heinemann.

Paulston, C. 1980. "The Sequencing of Structural Pattern Drills." In *Readings on English as a Second Language,* ed. K. Croft, 300–314. Cambridge, MA: Winthrop Publishers, Inc.

Peyton, J. K., ed. 1990. *Students and Teachers Writing Together: Perspectives on Journal Writing.* Alexandria, VA: Teachers of English to Speakers of Other Languages, Inc.

Piaget, J. 1977. *The Development of Thought: Equilibration of Cognitive Structure.* New York: Viking Press.

Raymond, D. 1989. "On Being 17, Bright and Unable to Read." In *Models for Writers: Short Stories for Composition,* eds. A. Rosa, and P. Escholz, 153–156. New York: St. Martin's Press.

Rief, L. 1992. *Seeking Diversity.* Portsmouth, NH: Heinemann.

Roy, C. 1989. "Features of Discourse in an American Sign Language Lecture." In *The Sociolinguistics of the Deaf Community,* ed. C. Lucas, 231–251. New York: Academic Press.

Rutherford, S. 1993. *A Study of American Deaf Folklore.* Burtonsville, MD: Linstok Press, Inc.

Sachar, L. 1993. *Marvin Redpost: Is He a Girl?* New York: Random House, Inc.

Sacks, O. 1989. *Seeing Voices.* Berkeley, CA: University of California Press.

Schleper, D. 1992. "When "F" Spells `Cat': Spelling in a Whole Language Program." *Perspectives in Education and Deafness* 11 (1): 11–14.

Schleper, D. 1996. "Talking About Books." *In Perspectives in Education and Deafness* 14 (3): 7–10.

Schor, S. 1990. "The Short, Happy Life of Ms. Mystery." In *Teaching at CUNY,* ed. M.J. Lederman, 32–42. New York: The City University of New York.

Schreiber, P. 1980. "On the Acquisition of Reading Fluency." *Journal of Reading Behavior* 12 (3): 177–186.

Shoemake, D. "Why Do We Teach 'Down' to Deaf Children?" *Silent News.* August 1992: 3.

Slobin, D. 1973. "Cognitive Prerequisites for the Development of Grammar." In *Studies of Child Language Development*, eds. C. Ferguson and D. Slobin, 175–208. New York: Holt, Rinehart & Winston.

Smith, F. 1986. *Insult to Intelligence.* New York: Arbor House.

Stadler, J. 1987. *Three Cheers for Hippo!* New York: Harper & Row Publishers.

Staton, J. 1985. "Using Dialogue Journals for Developing Thinking, Reading, and Writing with Hearing-impaired Students." In *Learning to Write and Writing to Learn,* ed. R. Kretschmer, 127–154. Washington, DC: The Alexander Graham Bell Association for the Deaf.

Staton, J. 1990. *Conversations in Writing: A Guide for Using Dialogue Journals with Deaf Postsecondary and Secondary Students.* Washington, DC: The Gallaudet Research Institute.

Stevenson, A. 1959. *Abraham Lincoln: The Great Emancipator.* New York: Macmillan.

Stewart, D. 1991. "ASL Intervention Strategies for Teachers." In *Advances in Cognition, Education, and Deafness,* ed. D. Martin, 356–361. Washington, DC: Gallaudet University Press.

Streng, A., R. Kretschmer, and L. Kretchmer. 1978. *Language, Learning, and Deafness. Theory, Application, and Classroom Management.* New York: Grune & Stratton.

Strong, M. 1988. "A Bilingual Approach to the Education of Young Deaf Children: ASL and English." In *Language Learning and Deafness,* ed. M. Strong, 113–129. Cambridge, MA: Cambridge University Press.

Supalla, S. 1986. *Manually Coded English: The Modality Question in Signed English.* Masters thesis, University of Illinois, Urbana-Champagne.

Suty, K., and S. Friel-Patti. 1982. "Looking Beyond Signed English to Describe the Language of Two Deaf Children." *Sign Language Studies* 35 (Summer): 153–166.

Svartholm, K. 1993. "Bilingual Education for the Deaf in Sweden." *Sign Language Studies* 81 (Winter): 291–332.

Togioka, P., J. Wolf, and C. Culbreath. 1994. "Using ASL and Videotaping in the Writing Process." In *Post Milan ASL & English Literacy: Issues, Trends, & Research,* ed. B. Snider, 75–90.Washington, DC: Gallaudet University, Continuing Education and Outreach.

Treiman, R., and K. Hirsh-Pasek. 1983. "Silent Reading: Insights from Second-Generation Deaf Readers." *Cognitive Psychology* 15(1): 39–65.

Trelease, J. 1989. *The New Read-Aloud Handbook.* New York: Penguin Books.

Trelease, J. 1992. *Hey! Listen to This: Stories to Read Aloud.* New York: Penguin Books.

Tripp, V. 1991a. *Meet Felicity.* Middleton, WI: Pleasant Company.

Tripp, V. 1991b. *Felicity Learns a Lesson.* Middleton, WI: Pleasant Company.

Tunmer, W., and Nesdale, A. 1985. "Phonemic Segmentation Skill and Beginning Reading." *Journal of Experimental Psychology* 77 (4): 417–427.

Valencia, S., and P.D. Pearson. 1987. "Reading Assessment: Time for a Change." *The Reading Teacher* 40 (8): 726–732.

Walmsley, S. 1994. *Children Exploring Their World: Theme Teaching in Elementary School.* Portsmouth, NH: Heinemann.

Wells, R. 1992. *Hazel's Amazing Mother.* New York: Puffin Books.

Williams, C. 1994. "The Language and Literacy Worlds of Three Profoundly Deaf Preschool Children." *Reading Research Quarterly* 29 (2): 125–155.

Wilton, S. 1993. "New Biographies are Better Than Before." In *Children's Literature and Social Studies: Selecting and Using Notable Books in the Classroom,* eds. M. Zarnowski and A. Gallagher, 16–19. Dubuque, IA: Kendall/Hunt Publishing Company.

Wolkomir, R. 1992. "American Sign Language: It's Not Mouth Stuff—It's Brain Stuff." *Smithsonian* 22(4): 30–41.

Young, T.A., and S. Vardell. 1993. "Weaving Readers Theatre and Non-Fiction into the Curriculum." *The Reading Teacher* 46 (5): 396–405.

Zarnowski, M. 1990. *Learning About Biographies: A Reading and Writing Approach for Children.* Urbana, IL: National Council of Teachers of English.

Appendix A

Suggested Books for Very Beginning Readers

Picture Books

Doyle, C. 1995. *Where's Bunny's Mommy?* New York: Simon & Schuster.

Hutchins, P. 1971. *Titch.* New York: Macmillan.

Jenson, P. 1990. *The Mess.* Chicago: Children's Press.

Krauss, R. 1945. *The Carrot Seed.* New York: Harper & Row.

Ormerod, J. 1992. *Come Back Kittens.* New York: Lothrop, Lee & Shepard Books.

Stadler, J. 1987. *Three Cheers for Hippo.* New York: Harper & Row.

Book Series

An I Can Read Book—Level 1—New York: Harper Trophy (A Division of Harper Collins) such as: *Who Will Be My Friends?.*

Hello Reader—Level 1—New York: Scholastic.

Puffin Easy to Read—Level 1—New York: Puffin Books (Published by the Penguin Group).

School Zone Start to Read Series—Level 1—Grand Haven, MI: School Zone Publishing Company.

Step into Reading: STEP 1—New York: Random House/Children's Television Workshop such as: *Happy Birthday, Cookie Monster!* and *Grover, Grover, Come on Over.*

Story Box Level 1, SET A. Bothell, WA: Wright Group.

Appendix B

Suggested Reading Series
for Beginning Older Readers
(Pre-teen and up)

Bookworm Series 1
Oxford University Press
198 Madison Avenue
New York, NY 10016

Connection Series
High Noon Books
20 Commercial Blvd., Suite 303
Novato, CA 94947-6191

Kaleidoscope Series
Timeless Tales Series
New Readers Press
Box 131
Syracuse, N.Y. 13210

Novels for Pleasure
Dominie Press
5945 Pacific Center Blvd., Suite 505
San Diego, CA 92121

Appendix C

Suggested Wordless Picture Books
for Beginning Readers in the Middle Grades

Collington, P. 1987. *The Angel and the Soldier Boy*. New York: Alfred A. Knopf.

Collington, P. 1990. *On Christmas Eve*. New York: Alfred A. Knopf.

DePaola, T. 1978. *Pancakes for Breakfast*. New York: Harcourt Brace & Company.

Goodall, J. 1978. *The Story of an English Village*. New York: Atheneum.

Krahn, F. 1975. *Who's Seen the Scissors?* New York: E.P. Dutton & Co., Inc.

Krahn, F. 1977. *A Funny Friend from Heaven*. New York: J.B. Lippincott Company.

Krahn, F. 1978. *The Great Ape*. New York: The Viking Press.

Krahn, F. 1985. *Amanda and the Mysterious Carpet*. New York: Clarion Books.

Mayer, M. 1977. *Frog Goes to Dinner*. New York: Dial Press.

Prater, J. 1986. *The Gift*. New York: Viking Penguin, Inc.

Schories, P. 1991. *Mouse Around*. New York: Farrar, Straus and Giroux.

Sis, P. 1992. *An Ocean World*. New York: Greenwillow.

Appendix D

Suggested Books for Adult Inexperienced Readers

Survival

Reid, P. 1974. *Alive.* New York: Avon.

Wiesel, E. 1958. *Night.* New York: Ballantine.

City Life and the Poor

Baldwin, J. 1974. *If Beale Street Could Talk.* New York: Dell Publishing, Inc.

Joravsky, B. 1995. *Hoop Dreams: A True Story of Hardship and Triumph.* Atlanta, GA: Turner Publishing, Inc.

Naylor, G. 1982. *The Women of Brewster Place.* New York: Penguin Books.

Thomas, P. 1967. *Down These Mean Streets.* New York: Vintage Books.

Interracial Relationships and Prejudice

Neufeld, J. 1968. *Edgar Allen.* New York: New American Library.

Gaines, E. 1971. *The Autobiography of Miss Jane Pittman.* New York: Bantam Books.

Wright, R. 1966. *Black Boy.* New York: Harper & Row.

Mathabane, M., and G. Mathabane. 1992. *Love in Black and White.* New York: HarperCollins.

Family Memoirs

Ashe, A., and A. Rampersad. 1993. *Days of Grace.* New York: Ballantine.

Delaney, S., and E. Delaney. 1993. *Having Our Say: The Delaney Sisters' First 100 Years.* New York: Dell Publishing.

Campbell, B. 1989. *Sweet Summer: Growing up With and Without My Dad.* New York: Ballantine Books.

Gilbreth, F., and E. Carey. 1948. *Cheaper by the Dozen.* New York: Bantam.

Walker, L. 1986. *A Loss for Words.* New York: Harper & Row.

War

Kovic, R. 1976. *Born on the Fourth of July.* New York: Pocket Books.

Mason, B. 1985. *In Country.* New York: Harper & Row.

Various Cultures, Various Lifestyles

Greenberg, J. 1970. *In This Sign.* New York: Henry Holt.

Greenberg, J. 1988. *Of Such Small Differences.* New York: Henry Holt.

Jacobs, L. 1980. *A Deaf Adult Speaks Out.* Washington, DC: Gallaudet University Press.

Mahmoody, B. 1987. *Not Without My Daughter.* New York: St. Martin's Press.

Mukherjee, B. 1975. *Wife.* New York: Fawcett Crest.

Mukherjee, B. 1989. *Jasmine.* New York: Fawcett Crest.

Addiction

Dorris, M. 1989. *The Broken Cord.* New York: Harper & Row.

Life in Apartheid South Africa

Mathabane, M. 1986. *Kaffir Boy: The True Story of a Black Youth's Coming of Age in Apartheid South Africa.* New York: New American Library.

Mathabane, M. 1994. *African Women: Three Generations.* New York: HarperCollins.

Crime and Punishment

Smith, D. 1994. *Beyond All Reason.* New York: Donald Fine, Inc.

Appendix E

Model Essays and Collections for Teaching Writing to Adult Inexperienced Writers

Cardello, M. 1993. "I Wish." In *The Writer's Craft*, eds. S. Gillespie, R. Becker, and R. Singleton, 147-148. New York: HarperCollins.

Cisneros, S. 1984. *House on Mango Street*. New York: Vintage Books.

Francke, L. 1993. "The Ambivalence of Abortion." In *The Writer's Craft*, eds. S. Gillespie, R. Becker, and R. Singleton, 47-50. New York: HarperCollins.

Garretson, M., ed. 1992. *Viewpoints on Deafness: A Deaf American Monograph*. Silver Spring, MD: The National Association of the Deaf.

Glickfeld, C. 1991. "What My Mother Knows." In *Connections: Using Multi-Cultural, Racial and Ethnic Short Stories to Promote Better Writing*, ed. S. Barber, 103-107. Dubuque, IA: Kendall/Hunt.

Mlynarczyk, R., and S. Haber. 1991. *In Our Own Words*. New York: St. Martin's Press.

Moseley, A., and J. Harris. 1994. *Interactions: A Thematic Reader*. Princeton, NJ: Houghton Mifflin.

Papashvily, G., and H. Papashivily. 1990. "Yes, Your Honesty." In *The Engaging Reader*, ed. A. King, 93-98. New York: Macmillan.

Rawlins, J. 1992. *The Writer's Way*. Princeton, NJ: Houghton Mifflin Company. (Try the student essays in this collection.)

Raymond, D. 1989. "On Being 17, Bright and Unable to Read." In *Models for Writers: Short Stories for Composition*, eds. A. Rosa and P. Eschholz, 153–156. New York: St. Martin's Press.

Silent News. 1425 Jefferson Road, Rochester, NY 14623-3139. (Try the *Editor's Note* and *Opinion* pages)

Soto, G. 1985. *Living Up the Street*. New York: Dell.

Voices of Deaf Student Writers: 20 Top Essays. 1995. Long Island City, NY: LaGuardia Community College, Program for Deaf Adults.

Weiner, H., and C. Bazerman. 1993. *Side by Side: A Multicultural Reader*. Boston, MA: Houghton Mifflin.

Appendix F

Resources for Children's Informational Picture Books

American Library Association. *Book Links.*
(A bimonthly publication that links books on a similar theme. The July issue includes an annual index. For subscriptions, write to *Book Links*, 434 W. Downer, Aurora, IL 60506.)

Braddon, K., N. Hall, and D. Taylor. 1993. *Math Through Children's Literature.* Englewood, CO: Teachers' Ideas Press.

California Department of Education. 1993. *Literature for History-Social Science: Kindergarten Through Grade Eight* (rev. ed.).
(Write to the Bureau of Publications, Sales Unit, California Department of Education, P.O. Box 271, Sacramento, CA 95812-0271.)

California Department of Education. 1993. *Literature for Science and Mathematics: Kindergarten Through Grade Twelve.* (See above for ordering information.)

Children's Book Council, Inc. *Notable Children's Trade Books in the Field of Social Studies.* New York: Children's Book Council.

Freeman, E.B., and D.G. Person. eds. 1992. *Using Nonfiction Trade Books in the Elementary Classroom: From Ants to Zeppelins.* Urbana, IL: National Council of Teachers of English.

Lima, C., and J. Lima. 1993. *A to Zoo: Subject Access to Children's Picture Books.* New Providence, NJ: R.R. Bowker.

Thiessen, D., and M. Matthias. 1993. *The Wonderful World of Mathematics: A Critically Annotated List of Children's Books in Mathematics.* Newark, DE: The International Reading Association.

Zarnowski, M., and A. Gallagher. 1993. *Children's Literature and Social Studies: Selecting and Using Notable Books in the Classroom.* Newark, DE: The International Reading Association.

Index